It would be nice to be able to say "It is Finished. There is now a Directory of Johnson Brothers patterns and with the exception of future patterns, my work is done." But, in reality, such a statement is far from the truth. This Directory is not the end of a project, but only the beginning.

All the patterns acknowledged in this book are included because they were located, occasionally just in print, but far more often by the presence of an actual piece in hand. Many more are out there, excluded solely because a piece has not been found. In the early years at Johnson Brothers, records were not kept past the period during which a specific pattern was active. As a result, names and other information on older patterns are literally impossible to find unless they extend within the memories of current or recent employees. Even as you read this, work continues on gathering more information and locating more of the older patterns as well as keeping up with the new ones. I wish to make an appeal to any and all who may have further knowledge of Johnson Brothers patterns. If you have something to add or if you find an error, please do not hesitate to contact me at the address below.

MARFINE ANTIQUES

Johnson Brothers Dinnerware Replacement Service

MARY FINEGAN
Owner
(704) 262-3441

Mailing Address:
P.O. Box 3618
Boone, N.C. 28607

This book is dedicated to my husband, Bob, whose knowledge of dinnerware is minimal, but whose knowledge of the highways and byways leading to antique fairs and flea markets is legion...

ACKNOWLEDGEMENTS

THANK YOU   THANK YOU   THANK YOU

A very special thanks is due to Mr. John Healings at the Johnson Brothers plant in England. The patience and endurance he displayed in seeking the answers to my never ending barrage of questions went well beyond the call of duty.

AND THANK YOU, TOO.........

Bill Brooks, Photographer	Atlanta, GA.
Fran Griffin, Layout & Design	Conover, N.C.
Gallens Antiques	College Park, GA.
Linda's Collectibles	Fayetteville, GA.
Boone Antique Mall	Boone, N.C.
Mid-America Tablewares	Eau Claire, WI.
Anne Finegan	Chicago, IL.
Barbara Finegan	Indianapolis, IN.
Donna Finegan	Chicago, IL.
Jay Finegan	Cleveland, OH.
Linden Simonson	Milwaukee, WI.
Ernestine Soller	Raleigh, N.C.
Darlene Wallace	Atlanta, GA.
Betty Beaty	Dallas, TX.
Richard Wojciechowski	Reading, PA.
David Griffiths	Cardiff, Wales, U.K.

CONTENTS

Chapter I
HISTORY & DEVELOPMENT OF POTTERY....................11

Chapter II
EARTHENWARE - STONEWARE - PORCELAIN..............15

Chapter III
FINISHING AND DECORATING..........................21

Chapter IV
JOHNSON BROTHERS..............................25

Chapter V
BITS & PIECES - TERMINOLOGY.....................31

Chapter VI
FLOW BLUE.......................................51

Chapter VII
SUGGESTED PRICING..............................55

Chapter VIII
PATTERN IDENTIFICATION..........................59

ORDER FORMS............................119 - 121

CHAPTER I

HISTORY AND DEVELOPMENT OF POTTERY

Although the origin of the word pottery is well known - it is derived from the Latin word "potum " which means " a pot " - the origin of the technique of pottery making is lost in antiquity. Ancient man had to eat, and from the beginning, implements had to be designed for the gathering, preparing, serving, and storing of food. The earliest pieces were undoubtedly stones or rocks occurring naturally in some usable form. Later, pieces of wood were carved and reeds were woven to produce vessels of a needed size and shape. In time, man learned that the molding and baking of "mud " would achieve even better results - an endless variety of sizes and shapes with decorative potential as well.

The earliest pieces of pottery were basically a mixture of clay and water, molded into the desired shape, and then dried in the sun over a long period of time. Later, the potter learned that baking the pieces in a hot fire not only reduced the drying time, but increased the strength of the piece as well. The final product resembled the terra cotta of our present day clay flower pots. These pieces, generally referred to as earthenware, were relatively durable and non-porous. Thousands of years later, further improvements were achieved through the development of an oven, or kiln, which not only allowed for the high temperatures needed, but also provided for the uniform access of heat to all sides and areas of a piece.

Until the Middle Ages, pottery making was a non-competitive business. Early potters lived near their clay supply and worked on a very small scale. Their wares were simple, designed according to the needs of the community and the talents of the potter, and still resembling the terra cotta of ancient times.

In the 1400's the Chinese were the first to begin producing

on a large scale, and as a natural outcome of mass production, to begin the exportation of pottery. In time, large pottery factories and centers were established in Europe, first in Germany, and later in England, Italy, and other countries. This expansion of the pottery industry, together with concurrent advances in transportation and communication, eventually led to intense rivalry and competition, complete with advertising and gimmickry. By the 1800's, the manufacturing of pottery had entered the world of "Big Business".

Throughout the years in which the Chinese led in the expansion of pottery manufacturing, they also pioneered new techniques in production and decorating. The Chinese were the first to develop porcelain, a much finer ware, which began to arrive in Europe at a time when the local potters were still at the terra cotta stage. From this it can be assumed that the word "china", as we use it today, was derived. Technically, the word "china" pertains to porcelain. However, when we refer to the china cabinets that hold our tablewares and the china departments in the stores where we buy our tablewares, the term is loosely used to represent all types of ceramic tableware.

Chinese porcelain was very expensive when it was originally exported, and attempting to duplicate that porcelain soon became a primary challenge to potters everywhere. If a piece was broken, replacement was literally impossible. In those instances where a replacement could be arranged, the waiting time was likely to be years. Thus, the local potters were under pressure to develop something similar, not only to reduce the cost, but also to offer some hope for simplifying replacements. Many of the famous early potters were involved in this quest, among them Josiah Wedg-wood and Josiah Spode II, both of England. Eventually, the English potters were not only able to duplicate porcelain, but they developed their own innovations such as the addition of bone ash to the basic components. Called "bone china", this form was pioneered by Josiah Spode II in the early 1800's.

Another of the challenges faced by the potters in the early

days of the competitive period was the search for "white" in the finished product. Depending on the base clay used, the background color after baking typically varied from beige to gray. Finally, in the 1700's, a practical process was developed for the production of truly "white" ware. Several more techniques followed, and in the mid 1800's, the period of "all-white" ware reached a peak which held its popularity until the end of the century.

A browse through almost any antique shop will show evidence of this white period. These are the pieces, usually ironstone, noted for their utility. They are heavy in weight and appearance with a minimum of decoration - knobs on lids, handles on holloware, or embossed flowers or vines trimming an edge or surface. There are platters, pitchers, tureens, and storage jars, as well as the basic place setting pieces.

At the time, the largest export market, especially for the English potters, was America. The heavy, durable, gleaming white pieces were a welcome contrast to the usual bleakness of the frontier home of the 1800's. "Even the poorest of rural families gladly put away their wooden trenches and redware to set their tables with spotless white."[1]

In the 1900's, patterns and colors regained their popularity and have remained so to this day, although styles and color preferences do change from time to time.

Pottery making, now called ceramics, is a major factor in contemporary life, ranging from the home crafter to the industrial giants such as Wedgwood and Noritake. In addition to tableware and decorative pieces, the world of ceramics includes bricks, floor and wall tiles, sanitary ware, insulation for electrical needs, and even the heat shields for the space program.

1. "A Second Look at White Ironstone"   Jean Weatherbee   1985
   Wallace & Homestead Book Company p.7

CHAPTER II

EARTHENWARE - STONEWARE - PORCELAIN

Basically, pottery can be divided into three groups. The first and simplest form is earthenware, a mixture of clay and water baked at a temperature of approximately 1000 degrees centigrade (1832^0 F). This produces the "flowerpot" type of ware and is used today mostly for decorative purposes.

The next to be developed, and the finest form, is porcelain. Porcelain is a mixture of a special clay and two other ingredients, feldspar and petuntse, both silicate minerals resulting from the decomposition of granite. It is fired at a very high temperature, 1300^0 C. - 1400^0 C. (2372^0 F. - 2552^0 F.) and is the most durable.

There are two types of porcelain, hard paste and soft paste. Of these, hard paste is considered to be the better. Hard paste finished products are more durable, not easily scratched, colder to the touch, and chip in a shell shape. They are translucent and have a characteristic ring when snapped with the fingers. Since the base of hard paste porcelain and the glaze have very similar compositions, they are often fired together with all the colors but the metallics already in place under the glaze. This drastically reduces the incidence of crazing. Bone china is a hard paste formula to which bone ash is added to lend both whiteness and translucency. The resulting wares are especially delicate in appearance, extremely durable, and are generally considered to be a step below true porcelain.

Soft paste porcelain has a glass-like appearance. Its composition is similar to that of hard paste except that the soft paste does not contain petuntse. It is not as durable, especially to extremes of temperature, and is more easily scratched. Soft paste porcelain is more suitable for decorative pieces than it is for tableware.

The third form, stoneware, was the last to be developed. Considered to be between earthenware and porcelain in quality, it is basically a type of earthenware with the addition of a variety of other materials and a higher baking temperature, near that of porcelain. This results in a product that possesses the best qualities of both. It is inexpensive as is earthenware, yet it has much of the durability of porcelain. Ironstone is the most prominent member in this category. It is a hard paste product which is dense and strong and resistant to chipping, qualities which have given ironstone its fitting name. Unlike porcelain, however, it is not translucent although it does have a vitrified, or glass-like, surface.

The components of ironstone vary considerably. Each company has its own "recipe" and even that is subject to variation as the different colors and patterns are produced. Clay is a basic ingredient, but after that there is a wide diversity in the components used, kaolin in some, flint (a hard quartz), and silica (found in sand) in others. In the early days, "slag" from the iron furnaces was included in the formula for greater strength and durability. Slag is essentially a collection of waste products which floats to the top in the smelting process. It is not used today at the Johnson Brothers plant, but it may be a component of the ironstone of other manufacturers since formulas are secret and guarded. But even if it is no longer in use by anyone, the fact that it was used at all does give further credence to the name of *"ironstone"*. Although various types of stoneware, including some crude types of ironstone, were manufactured throughout the 1700's, the development of ironstone most similar to that which we know today is attributed to the J.C. Mason & Company of England, who took out a patent on their product in 1813. The body of that product did contain pulverized slag as one of the ingredients.

In the production of ironstone tablewares, the clay and water and any other components are thoroughly mixed, resulting in a soupy mixture called *slip*. This in turn is placed in large filter presses where the water is squeezed out until the mixture is easily workable. It is then divided into small packets, called *bats,* which are either molded by hand or placed on molding machines which are modern versions of the potters wheel. For some holloware items, slip is poured into plaster of paris molds which shape the pieces as water is absorbed. After the molding and shaping process, trim and appendages are added and the pieces continue to dry. They are called *"greenware"* at this point.

When the proper dryness has been reached, the pieces are placed in a kiln for the first firing. Just as advancements have occurred in other types of industry, so too, the modern day techniques of production in the pottery industry are far removed from the early methods of even those of fifty years ago. Early industrial kilns were usually of the bottle type, a broad round base with a tall central chimney. The wood or coal fired furnace was in the center, and the wares to be baked were placed in containers, called *saggers*, all around the sides. These racks were stacked in concentric rings, up to 16 feet high, until the oven was filled. All of the loading and stacking was done by hand, and a large oven might contain as many as 2000 saggers. Later, when the firing time was completed, the oven had to cool before the workers could enter and begin removing the saggers. Following the first firing, the pieces, which were musty green before, are now white in color and are called *biscuitware.*

The entire firing process was under the control of one man, the fireman. He alone was responsible for this most critical part of the production cycle, and an error on his part could result in a disastrous financial loss. He was the most respected employee at the plant, and it was his job to stay with his kiln from the initial fire-up to the beginning of the cool-down, often for days at a time. His goal was an oven temperature of 1000° C. - 1200° C. (1832° F. - 2192° F.), and he had to achieve this goal by experience alone. He had only the color of the flame and the porosity of pieces periodically drawn from the oven as his guides. He controlled the oven through the addition of fuel and through the opening and closing of dampers built into the top and sides of the oven. In *" THE POT-TERIES"*, David Sekers writes: "After kindling the firemouths, the fireman had to stay up with each oven, often for 72 hours on end - a job which gave firemen a proverbial thirst. An average size biscuit oven could consume in that period 10 to 12 tons of coal. The fireman had to control each firemouth and judge when to increase ventilation or temperature and when to leave well enough alone. How much beer an average fireman consumed is not recorded."[1]

Another, less popular early kiln was the beehive type. This oven was a shorter, mound-type structure with a chimney stack alongside. It was developed later than the bottle type and was most often used for the manufacture of bricks and quarry tiles.

Following World War II, the pottery industry in Britain began an intensive modernization program. Kilns are now "tunnel" kilns, fueled by gas or electricity, and designed with varying temperatures in different areas. Cars or trolleys are loaded at one end and move through the different zones so that when they emerge at the opposite end 48 hours later, the cycle is completed and cooling is well under way. The process is continuous. As soon as a trolley is unloaded at the far end, it is reloaded and attached to the "train" at the beginning in order to start the cycle all over again.

As the pottery industry grew in centers such as "The Potteries" area of Britain, a most undesirable side effect grew with it - atmospheric pollution. In years past, clouds of smoke from the hundreds of kilns literally blotted out the sun, and it has been said that picture taking was reserved for holiday weeks when factories were shut down. Living and working conditions were deplorable, characterized by long hours, extremes of temperature, and poor sanitation. In addition to the serious lung problems from the smoke pollution and flint dust, a second health problem was

1. THE POTTERIES, David Sekers, Shire Publications, Ltd. p. 25

prevalent. This was lead poisoning from the glazes. Today, dangerous lead glazes are no longer in use, and pictures may be taken any day, weather permitting.

CHAPTER III

FINISHING AND DECORATING

The very earliest potters had to do all their decorating by hand. Bats of clay were molded, pressed, pinched, and ridged with the fingers. Occasionally, a "tool" was used to achieve a specific result - a sharp stick for incising a design or a shell for imprinting an image. Later, when the potter's wheel was developed to aid in the shaping of round bowls and jugs, surface decoration was still a hand craft.

The use of color as a form of decoration has been known since the pre-Christian era. Not only was color variation achieved through the use of different clays as bases, but a range of colors and hues was produced by the addition of chemicals to the glazes as well. Evidence has shown that the early Assyrians used copper in the glaze for green, cobalt for blue, and manganese for purple. Additionally, other chemicals were used to alter the translucency of the glaze, allowing for variation from clear and glossy to opaque white.

Hand painting, as a form of decoration, was used by the Chinese on their porcelain long before the technique was adopted by the rest of the world. Although a variety of colors was used on the surface of the glaze, only blue, derived from cobalt, was used for underglaze painting. This was the only color that was able to withstand the high temperature of the glost (glaze) firing. In time, other usable underglaze paints were developed so that today, an extensive range of colors and shades is available.

One can still find contemporary pieces of onglaze painting, although such pieces are usually for decorative purposes. Surface painting is not as practical for tableware as is underglaze decoration since without a glass-like cover, it is not as durable under the constant wear and frequent washings required. Several of the earlier patterns produced by Johnson Brothers do have onglaze decoration. These onglaze decorated pieces should never be placed in a dishwasher and should be handwashed with care.

Occasionally, plates that were manufactured as plain white (or possibly a solid color) are used by artists to apply their talent. In my personal collection, I have a white, scallop-edge Johnson Brothers plate edged in gold. In the center is a lovely onglaze spray of violets. The artist, Stella Walker, will be pleased to know that her beautiful plate has been the recipient of many compliments.

The pottery industry took a giant step forward when the transfer printing process was developed in the late 1700's. Basically, this is a system of applying a design through the use of paper imprinted with the desired image by an *engraving*. An engraving is a copper plate on which tiny lines and dots are tooled, forming the picture. On a pattern produced from an engraving, that which appears as a solid color, is actually a series of tiny markings so numerous and so closely placed that the final printing gives the impression of one solid mass of color.

The original engravings were produced on flat copper plates. A sheet of prepared tissue was laid in place over the plate, pressure was applied through a roller press, and the image appeared on the tissue. The tissue was quickly cut in sections for ease of fitting and then applied to the ware while the ink was still wet. When the paper was removed, the design remained. In the mid-thirties, the process was improved and accelerated through the installation of printing machines. Rather than flat plates of copper, the designs are worked onto copper rollers which print long streams of tissue paper. This offers a ready supply of pattern designs which can be stored in dry form until needed.

At the time of application, the desired pattern is cut into separate sections which are moistened and literally "molded" by hand to the biscuitware piece. Care must be taken to match edges of design and borders as closely as possible, and though, on some pieces this process is relatively simple, on other pieces such as a teapot, the placing and matching can be quite a challenge. Once the pattern is in place, the piece is rubbed and pressed to transfer the image.

When the design from the engraving is set, the piece is immersed in water. The tissue floats off, leaving the image in place. A low temperature baking of 800^0 C. (1472^0 F.) usually follows to remove the oils and harden the color before further decoration or glazing.

If further color is to be applied, it is usually done by individual hand painting or through the use of modern technology such as the new multi-color printing machine. Although some handcoloring of an already printed pattern continues at Johnson Brothers, it is too costly and too time-consuming to be a part of today's general manufacturing process. In time, all such work will be done through technology.

Further improvements and acceleration in the technique of transfer printing were realized in the late 1950's with the development of a new semi-automatic decorating machine called the Murray Curvex. A print is transferred from a flat engraving onto a gelatin pad. The pad is inked and then stamped onto the flatter pieces of biscuitware. Since the gelatin is soft and somewhat flexible, it molds itself to the shape of the piece. This method is used today for plates, fruits, and cereals, but the hand application of tissue designs is still needed for holloware pieces such as teapots, sugars, creamers, and cups.

The use of slipware is another form of decorating ceramic pieces. In this method, clay and water are mixed to the desired consistency and painted or molded onto a surface in a decorative design. Wedgwood's "Jasperware" is one form of this type of decorating. Alternatively, designs are scratched into added slip, to expose the different color of the original piece underneath.

Decorating through the use of lithographs or decals is commonly chosen when the design is mainly a border. The decal is moistened and applied to the appropriate area, after which the biscuitware is refired. The background of the decal fires away, leaving the design in place.

Whether a piece of biscuitware is left plain or is decorated by one or more of the methods discussed, the final step in decorating of tableware is the application of a glaze followed by a glost firing. A *glaze* is a coating applied in order to give the ware a shiny, glass-like surface. It is not essential since stoneware is in itself non-porous. But it enhances the appearance, seals in and preserves any underglaze decorating, and promotes ease in cleaning.

One of the earliest forms of glaze on stoneware was the salt glaze, introduced in the 1600's. A handful of salt was thrown into the kiln. The salt vaporized and settled in minute droplets, eventually forming a thin, all-over coating, pitted in appearance. Salt glaze was, and is, most often used on various forms of crockery.

Until the 20th century, the glaze of choice was the liquid lead glaze. The biscuitware was dipped into the solution and then re-fired. This liquid glaze was a raw lead compound that led to many health problems and even death from the resulting lead poisoning. Today, a "fritted" lead product is used. It may be either in liquid form, which is used for dipping or brushing, or in powder form, which is sprayed onto the wares. Fritted lead is produced by melting lead in with other glaze materials. It is not dangerous to health as was the raw lead form.

Following the application of the glaze compound, the wares are placed in racks in such a way that they are separated from touching by resting on spurs, stilts, or pins. The glost firing is at a lower temperature 1000^0 C.-1040^0 C. or (1832^0 F.-1904^0 F.), determined primarily by the composition of glaze material and the number and nature of the colors used.

Customers occasionally ask about the small rough blemishes, usually three, on the backside of a plate or bowl. These spots occur as a result of being supported on pins during the glazing process. They are not defects and in no way detract from the value of the piece, even though some staining of the tiny areas may occur in time.

CHAPTER IV

JOHNSON BROTHERS

The first of what were to become Johnson Brothers factories had been functioning in the manufacture of tableware long before the brothers entered the business in 1883. The plant, called the Charles Street Works, was located in Hanley, the largest of six towns which later joined together to form the city of Stoke-on-Trent. This city is in the district of Staffordshire and is near the western coast of middle England, a region generally known for its industry and manufacturing. The Stoke area was ideal for the development of the pottery industry, for most of the essential raw materials were readily available. There was clay for the manufacture of earthenware and coal for heating the furnace right in the area, while relatively close by were the lead and salt needed for the glazing. An added advantage was the proximity of the sea. Stoke-on-Trent is less than 60 miles from the major shipping port of Liverpool, and in the early part of the 18th century, a series of canals and locks was built to transport the wares on barges to the port, providing a much smoother and safer ride for such wares than a trip on the early roads would have been. Today, Johnson Brothers still has two of the barges in use though most of the other manufacturers have discontinued the practice. These two vessels are no longer used for trips to the coast, but operate on a $1\frac{1}{2}$ mile stretch of waterway to transport the wares from the manufacturing sites at Hanley to a storage and distribution base, a 15 minute cruise away. A fleet of trailer trucks then carries the goods throughout the country.

William Mallor, the original owner, established the plant at the top of Charles Street in 1758. His business continued there until 1804 when it became Keeling and Company. Four other pottery businesses followed in rapid succession. The last of these was J.W. Pankhurst who took over the plant in 1862 and continued in the production of tableware, mainly whiteware intended for export to the United States. In 1882, the J.W. Pankhurst Company declared bankruptcy and the business was sold at a receiver's sale. The buyers were Alfred, Frederick, and Henry Johnson, and the partnership they formed was called Johnson Brothers. These three young men were not new to business, for their father had married the daughter of a Master Potter (one of the Meakin girls), and they had learned their trade well in their maternal grandfather's factories.

In 1883 production began, mainly the whiteware still so popular at the time. Within a few years, the company introduced a new underglaze printed ware, distinguished by lighter weight and finer finish than was usual at the time. It still maintained a high degree of durability while it had the thinness and delicacy of porcelain. For a time, the term "Semi-Porcelain" was even included in the backstamp. It was prettier, with considerable color, and best of all, it was inexpensive. It is this quality ironstone which has been, and still is, the mainstay of the Johnson Brothers Tableware business.

The company prospered. In 1896, a fourth brother, Robert, joined the firm, bringing his specialty of marketing and selling. Robert lived and worked in the United States, concentrating his talents on expanding the U. S. market for Johnson Brothers products. By 1914, Johnson Brothers owned and operated five additional factories, four of them producing tableware, and the fifth, Trent Pottery, producing sanitary ware. All of these plants were in "The Potteries" area, two within walking distance of the original Charles Street Works.

Eventually, the four original Johnson brothers either retired or moved on to other areas, and the sons of the founders became involved. Most of the Johnson's families were large, and by the second generation it became necessary to establish a policy whereby only two sons from each family could come permanently into the business. Other members could be trained there but would have to leave to go into business elsewhere. Several of the sons did join in, and one of Robert's sons followed in his father's footsteps by taking over the American market after his father's death in 1909.

Throughout the early twentieth century, the business continued to grow until the outbreak of World War I in 1914. With so many of the work force in the Armed Services and the difficulties of shipping abroad, business was severely curtailed. But as soon as the war was over, production and sales quickly geared up, and the twenties and thirties saw many improvements and innovations in both design and color. Many of the techniques and patterns still popular today had their origins in this period. The *"Dawn"* series was developed, a new concept of a colored body so that when a chip occurs in one of these pieces, it shows the same color throughout, not just painted on the surface of a white body. In addition, a new ivory colored body was developed, the off-white *"Pareek"* still in use today, and the ever popular patterns *"Old Britain Castles"* and *"Historic America"* were introduced. Markets continued to expand, and the Johnson Brothers Company earned an outstanding reputation both at home and abroad.

The onset of World War II in 1939 brought development to a halt and severely restricted production just as World War I had done in 1914. The company struggled through this second most difficult period, even managing occasional shipments to overseas markets. By this time the grandsons of the founders were in the business though most of them were called to military service and did not assume leadership roles until after the war was over.

In 1946, a massive expansion and modernization program began. New gas fired tunnel kilns were built in all of the factories, replacing the old bottle kilns. This project had been started just prior to World War II, but it had to be curtailed after only one tunnel kiln had been built. In 1947, a tableware manufacturing plant in Hamilton, Ontario, Canada was purchased and was used for some time afterward as a "decorating" unit. Today, no longer a part of Johnson Brothers, it functions in the processing and distribution of tiles. In 1957, one of the grandsons, Stephen, left for Australia where he set up a tableware manufacturing plant at Croydon, near Melbourne. The Croydon plant was in operation for many years, supplying a large portion of the tableware requirements in that regional market. It was closed down in 1985. In 1960 and 1965, two more local plants were purchased, one of which, the former J. G. Meakin, Ltd. plant, is used primarily for the decorating and glost (glaze) firing of biscuitware manufactured in some of the other nearby plants. The other is used for both the manufacture of tableware and gift-ranges and as a centralized carton packing and dispatch operation.

Modernization and expansion continue in the high-tech area as well. Computers are now in use, not only for the usual record keeping, but also in the actual manufacturing process, such as controlling slip preparation recipes in order to promote consistent quality. A new multi-color printing system has been developed to assure more uniformity in coloring, while saving both time and expense. Even the long standing technique of decorating from engravings has been updated by the Murray-Curvex machine which mechanizes the time consuming process of applying patterns to biscuitware by hand.

Johnson Brothers was among the first winners of the *Queen's Award to Industry* for export achievement. This is an award granted by the Queen in recognition of a consistent high level of exports as compared to total sales. At the time, the company had reached an export level of 70% of total sales. This award was received in 1966 and again in 1971. Today, the home market has increased so that the percentage of wares exported is considerably less.

In 1968, Johnson Brothers became part of the Wedgwood Group in order to combine resources and promote business interests. Other ceramic manufacturers also included in this group are Coalport, Adams, Meakin, Midwinter, Crown Staffordshire, and Masons. For several years Johnson Brothers, while also selling other brands, functioned under the name "Creative Tableware", with its "Bull in a China Shop" logo. But in 1991, a re-launch of the Johnson Brothers name took place. The china shop image is now gone, replaced by a more formal looking Royal Warrant symbol with a much less prominent bull underneath.

At the time of the Wedgwood merger, two of the fourth generation Johnsons, Christopher and Robert, continued in management as members of the Main Board of the Wedgwood Company. Today, Robert is still serving as Managing Director of Johnson Brothers which was, and still is, the largest single earthenware manufacturing concern in British history. Approximately 1500 employees produce more than 800,000 pieces weekly. Another change took place in 1986 when Waterford Glass PLC of Ireland merged with Wedgwood PLC of England. In the United States, this huge corporation is known as Waterford-Wedgwood USA and has based its headquarters in New Jersey.

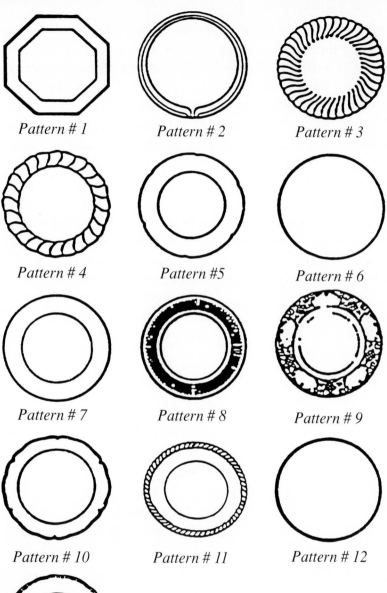

Pattern # 1 *Pattern # 2* *Pattern # 3*

Pattern # 4 *Pattern #5* *Pattern # 6*

Pattern # 7 *Pattern # 8* *Pattern # 9*

Pattern # 10 *Pattern # 11* *Pattern # 12*

Pattern # 13

FIGURE 1
Plate Shapes and Styles

CHAPTER V

BITS AND PIECES - TERMINOLOGY

1. <u>STYLE NUMBERS</u> - The style number offered with each of the patterns refers to Figure 1 (*opposite page*) where 13 styles are depicted. This style refers to the plate only. In recent years, many brochures have been printed on Johnson Brothers patterns showing silhouette or line drawing figures of various styles, ranging from the plate through the hollow ware pieces. (*See Fig. 2 pgs. 42-43*). These charts may apply to the newer patterns in this book but should not be assumed for the older ones, especially the pre-1930 patterns. Even in the newer patterns, there are some differences such as two different cup styles in the *"Indian Tree"* and *"Old Britain Castles"* patterns.

2. <u>BACKSTAMPS</u> - The backstamps can be used only as a general guide for dating a pattern. Written records were not kept until recent times. Therefore, when dealing with older patterns, back-stamps are dated based primarily on similarity to other backstamps of the era as well as style and color of the pattern. Kovel's "NEW DICTIONARY OF MARKS", Crown, offers four styles with approximate dating. (*See Fig. 3 on pg. 44*). Five others have been used, three of them recently and two of them in the early years (*Fig. 4 on pg. 44*) and (*Fig. 5 on pg. 45*). In addition to the Johnson Brothers backstamp, a pattern name may or may not be included. Cups, however, are not marked with a pattern name nor in most cases, even a Johnson Brothers backstamp. Occasionally, one may find cups with no markings at all, but usually, "Made in England" is etched into the base.

Customers have often asked about the dots and dashes of color on the back of a piece, usually near the backstamp. This is the "signature" of the artist who painted the various colors onto the imprinted pattern. Since some patterns are in production

31

30 years or more, the symbols may represent more than one individual artist.

With the introduction of a new multi-color printing machine, such hand painting is rapidly becoming a technique of the past so that the colored dots and dashes will rarely be seen on future pieces.

3. PIECES AVAILABLE - The list of pieces in *Figure 8 (pg. 48)* is representative of the pieces available in most of the Johnson Brothers patterns in the United States today. But this list is only a sampling of the more than 60 different items the company produces. Eating habits and traditions of countries throughout the world are studied and catered to, and the items manufactured range from huge turkey platters to tiny butterpats.

In years past, the assortment of pieces available was much greater than it is today. In the United States, the sets often included 9" luncheon plates as well as 10" dinner plates and 8" salads. Cereal bowls were available in round, square, and rimmed. A choice (of soup bowls) was offered, including not only the usual round and square, but also lug soups ("tab" handles at opposite ends), coupe soups (wide and shallow round bowls), rimmed soups, and cream soups (2-handled). I recently found some berry bowls with a three quarter inch rim. The dealer who sold me these bowls had purchased them in England where, he reported, they were quite common and were called "stone-fruits". After the stone containing fruits (e.g. prunes, apricots) were eaten, the stones were placed along the rim. Platters and serving bowls were produced in a variety of shapes and sizes as well.

Figure 7 on pgs. 46 & 47 is a copy of the original piece list for the pattern *"Royal Homes"*. This list was located at the Johnson Brothers plant in England and was compiled at the time of production of that pattern. It can be noted that many of the factory descriptions are very different from those we know in the United States. For example, "oval dishes" refers to platters while "round scallops" refers to open round vegetable bowls. Also, the sizes of the various plates are factory "trade" sizes and not the actual "measured" sizes. Thus, the "flat 4" plate" would have been the American bread and butter plate which normally measures 6 to 6¼". Also note the five different sizes of plates and platters and the three different sizes of teapots and coffeepots.

Occasionally, a really special piece in one of the more recent patterns can be found. One such item is a ginger jar. I have only seen one, in the *"Indian Tree"* pattern, but ginger jars in *"Rose Chintz"* and *"Old Britain Castles"* are also available.

In the *"Historic America"* series, jumbo-giant cups and saucers were produced as a novelty. These cups resemble small punch bowls, measuring 4½" high and 9¼" in diameter across the top. The saucer is 11¼" in diameter. I have located these sets in three of the color variations.

You may come upon a tab-handled plate approximately the same size as a regular dinner plate. This is an older English version of a bread and butter plate. In the United States, the bread and butter plate is a small side plate intended for use in each place setting. In England, the large plate was set in the center of the table and piled high with bread and butter. Today, a rectangular Sandwich Tray is more commonly used for this purpose in England.

In some patterns a 7" plate, midway between the 6" bread and butter and the 8" salad, may be found. This is the "tea" plate, the size used to serve pastries for the English mid-afternoon tea time. This is not to be confused with some of the newer patterns, especially the Style # 10 *(See Fig. 1 on pg. 30)* such as *"Berries"* or *"Provincial"* in which the regular bread and butter plate is larger than usual, also 7" in diameter. Occasionally square "tea" plates are seen. These pieces are identical in shape to the square salads but are 6" across rather than the 8" of the salad plates.

Through the years, Johnson Brothers has produced a variety of special serving pieces, ranging from a three-tiered upright piece, often found in *"Harvest Time"*, to a flat, three compartment Christmas Tree shaped piece found in both *"Merry Christmas"* and *"Friendly Village"*. In addition, a single Christmas Tree shape relish is available in both of these patterns, and a 2-tiered server is available in *"Twelve Days of Christmas"* and *"Friendly Village"*.

In the 1980's a new concept of marketing was introduced at Johnson Brothers - a variety of kitchen and linen items to match a specific tableware pattern. For some time, glassware to match the *"Friendly Village"* pattern had been available, but beginning with the pattern *"Eternal Beau"*, a wide range of products with matching designs entered the market. Later, *"Summer Chintz"*, *"Summerfields"*, and *"Fresh Fruit"* were expanded to include this coordinating line of products. In these patterns a host of round and oval baking dishes is available. Called *"A la Carte Cookware"*, these pieces are designed to go from freezer to oven to table. In addition, matching table linens are now available as well as miscellaneous giftware and accessory pieces, ranging from glassware, vases and planters to clocks, canisters and cutlery. It is even possible to match your bed linens, window shades and wallpaper to your tableware pattern today.

4. <u>BREAKFAST SETS</u> - Called *"Early Morning Sets"* in England, these sets were available in most of the more popular patterns up to the late 50's or early 60's. They were designed to serve two people, and in addition to the basic place setting pieces, included four unique serving pieces - a miniature sugar bowl, creamer, and coffee pot, and a toast or "muffin" cover sized to fit a standard round 8" plate. The complete set consisted of two cereal bowls, two cups and saucers, two eggcups, two 8" round plates for the place settings and a third as the muffin server, the muffin cover, and the miniature coffee set. Since the place setting pieces are the same as those from the dinnerware sets, one would have no way of knowing its origin when such a piece is found. But finding one of the miniature pieces or the muffin cover is really a special treat.

5. <u>OLD ENGLISH</u> - The term *"Old English"* on the back of a piece does not indicate the pattern name, but rather denotes a style. These pieces have the wide flat rims with a "rope" or piecrust edging. This style is found on patterns ranging from the 1920's or 30's (e.g. *"Guildford"*), up to the early 1970's (e.g. *"Devonshire"*). A pattern name may or may not be included in the backstamp. A resurgence of this style occurred in 1991 in the pattern *"Old English - White "*. However, in this new version, the "rope" edge is on the sovereign style plate (# 5) rather than on the classic style (# 7) as in the earlier patterns (*See Fig. 1 on pg. 30*). Patterned variations in this new style are expected to follow shortly.

6. <u>PAREEK</u> - The term *"Pareek"* on the back of a piece does not indicate the pattern name but rather denotes the background or base coloring. "Pareek" means off-white, typically a cream or very light beige color. Often the difference is not noted until a piece is placed next to a truly white (or "Snowhite") piece. This term is usually found stamped on patterns from the 1920's to the late 50's, although this base color is still in use today (e.g.*"Friendly Village"*). A pattern name may or may not be included in the backstamp. If a piece is stamped with "Pareek" without a further pattern name, it is most probably a painted onglaze decoration and should be hand washed only.

7. <u>TABLE PLUS</u> - *"Table Plus"* is the Johnson Brothers name for their freezer to table line. These wares are designed to withstand freezing, refrigeration, and oven use, both conventional and microwave. However, certain precautions are suggested. These include not placing a piece directly on a hot stove burner or flame, allowing for defrosting of contents before placing a dish in the oven, and making sure the bottom surface is sufficiently covered by liquid to evenly distribute heat when a piece is used over an alcohol burner or canned heat. Examples of patterns in this series are *"Papaya"* and *"Brandywine"*. "Table Plus" pieces are very

heavy, resembling the old style crockery in thickness and weight.

8. <u>OLD GRANITE</u> - The *"Old Granite"* series consists of a number of patterns, all in a country casual style and all on a "granite" or speckled base. The background color is usually a beige, ranging from a tan or yellow-beige, to a rosy beige, to a greenish tinge beige. In the patterns of this series, more than in any of the other patterns, variations in the background shadings of the different lots or batches are found. *"Fruit Sampler"*, especially, is extremely difficult to match, apparently due to its popularity and the quantity of lots produced through the years.

9. <u>WINDSORWARE</u> - *"WindsorWare"* is the tradename of a special range of Johnson Brothers patterns shipped to the Fisher Bruce Company of Philadelphia. This company was an importer/wholesaler which dealt mainly in patterns manufactured exclusively for them. Occasionally, pieces in this line can be found with a U. S. Patent Office mark, presumably registered and obtained by the Fisher Bruce Company itself. A regular pattern name may or may not be included in the backstamp. Two examples from this group are *"Garden Bouquet"* and *"Pomona"*. The WindsorWare line began in the 1940's and was discontinued in the early 1970's after Johnson Brothers became a part of the Wedgwood Group.

Due to the large number of unnamed WindsorWare patterns and to the popularity of these patterns, I felt it necessary to choose names for some of the more active ones in order to facilitate record keeping. When I have done so, it will be indicated in the Identification Section.

10. <u>COMMEMORATIVE PLATES</u> - One can often find commemorative plates with a Johnson Brothers backstamp. Usually, these plates were manufactured specifically for a particular business, most often a retail operation. Among those I have found are

"Chicago" produced for the Marshall Field & Company of Chicago, Illinois, the *"Oregon Plate"* produced for the Meier and Frank & Company of Portland, Oregon, and *"Mt. Rushmore"*, produced for the Sunset Supply Company of Rapid City, South Dakota. Other commemorative plates are available, including *"The Arizona Plate"*, *"Empire State Plate"*, and *"Great States of California"*. Most of these plates were manufactured in a variety of colors, including pink, blue, and brown. I have even seen a multicolor version of one of them.

11. <u>ROYAL WARRANTS</u> - *"Royal Warrants"* are honorary awards given by royalty to manufacturers of wares supplied to the Royal Households of "Her Majesty the Queen" and also "Her Majesty, Queen Elizabeth, the Queen's Mother". Johnson Brothers first became Royal Warrant holders in 1970 and have remained holders of these prestigious awards ever since. A special backstamp can be found on some, but not all, pieces of those patterns so honored *(See Fig. 6 on pg. 45)*. Two examples of Royal Warrant patterns are *"Coaching Scenes"* and *"Old Bradbury"*. These awards are not presented for each chosen pattern, but rather for consistent good quality and customer service over a number of years.

12. <u>COLORS</u> - Although 100 plus years of production has led to a variety of colors and hues in use, Johnson Brothers have been relatively consistent in the shades it used in the last sixty years. The most consistent is pink, not a true pink, but more of a rose color, often called red by the customers. When patterns using this color are compared side by side, the color seems to be the same on all. But in some patterns it appears "pink", whereas in others, the first impression is indeed "red". For the sake of uniformity, I am referring to this color as "pink" in all of the patterns in this book.

Most of the blue appears to be the same shade, a softened version of royal blue. But, there is a definite change to pastel in the pattern *"Hyde Park - Blue"*.

The mulberry color used is a deep plum color. In the early years of production of the *"Old Britain Castles"* pattern, another "lavender" shade was used although this pattern is seen in the deeper mulberry shade as well. Whereas, the mulberry shade has a great deal of red in it, the lavender tends more towards blue. To date, *"Old Britain Castles"* is the only pattern I have found in lavender. The Mulberry shade can be found on several patterns, among them *"Elizabeth"*, *"Old Mill"* and *"Enchanted Garden"*.

Green is used by Johnson Brothers in several shades. There is olive green (*"English Chippendale"*), true green (*"Vintage"*), and a deep aqua or teal color (*"Pastorale"*). Another version of green, mixed with gray and brown, is often used as a border color (e.g. transfer printing patterns). Two examples of this are *"Friendly Village"* and *"Millstream"*.

13. OLD BRITAIN CASTLES - AUTHENTICITY:

While on a trip to England in 1988, my husband and I decided to do a little research on the *"Old Britain Castles"* pattern. We chose that one because each design is dated as well as labeled, the date indicating the time of the original engraving from which the Johnson Brothers version was taken. Also, it had been called to our attention that the picture on the small 12" platter (Cambridge 1792) had a most unusual depiction on it. In front of the building and across an expanse of grounds, a barge being pulled down a canal (the River Ouse) by a horseteam is portrayed *(See Fig. 9 pg. 49)*. But, in this instance, the horses are in the water, whereas the usual method at the time was for the horses to be walking along the banks. We were curious about this, so we decided to see what we could find out.

At the Johnson Brothers plant in Stoke-on-Trent we learned that the drawings for the patterns to be used for *"Old Britain Castles"* were done in 1928 by a Miss Fennel, the daughter of a Master Engraver, who used book photographs of old steel engravings as guides. Her father's company was commissioned to produce the engravings. A team of about 10 engravers began the project in 1929, and worked on it for over a year. In 1930, the approximately forty engravings they produced were used to begin production of the original *"Old Britain Castles"* item range.

However, no one at Johnson Brothers could offer an explanation as to why the horses were in the water. All agreed that the usual practice was for the teams to be on the banks.

Our next stop was the Library at Cambridge itself. Our presence there caused quite a stir when it was learned that we were there to find out why the horses were in the water. With the help of the library personnel we were able to locate a picture printed from the original engraving, literally identical to the picture on the platter, with the exception of a few figures eliminated on the left side - and the horses *were* in the water! The writing under the engraving stated, "Engraved by J.W. Walker, from an original drawing by J.W. Walker. Figures by Burney. Published February 1, 1793 by J. Walker".

After looking through a few books on the History of River Navigation, we finally found our answer in one of them, *"The Great Ouse"*. We read the following: "The horses were criticized for walking, not at the summit, but on the slopes of the banks....... The resulting damage was appalling".[1] And "The watermen working on the Cam and Great Ouse traditionally were supposed to have a greater fund of bad language than had those of any other river in England; or alternatively this was thrown into greater prominence by association with the rarified academic atmosphere of Cambridge. Navigation through Cambridge, where bridges and buildings constituted recurring obstacles, could hardly have been more effectively designed to elicit extremes of language......The rough appearance, conduct and language of the watermen came

1. "The Great Ouse": History of a River Navigation, Dorothy
   Summers, Pub. David and Charles   1973   p. 90

under perpetual fire from the university authorities".[1] Eventually, a solution satisfactory to both sides was worked out - the building of a midstream roadway. "The presence of a gravel causeway on the river bed somewhat assisted their progress and it is thought to have been put there by the watermen for this very purpose. The inconvenience suffered by the colleges and the Navigation seems to have been mutual".[2] This is why the horses are pictured in the water on the small *"Old Britain Castles"* platter. On a scale of 1 to 10, the authenticity of at least this one design rates a 10.

14. <u>CRAZING</u> - *"Crazing"* is described as cracks in the surface of the glaze. It ranges from a single tiny line to all-over crackling, a mosaic of irregular sections. Occasionally, the lines will appear to be colored a dark brown. Normally, this indicates that the piece has been exposed to extreme heat, such as an oven, or has been stained by liquids, such as coffee. More often, the cracks are colorless, readily seen on plain backgrounds, but difficult to find within intricate patterns.

      Crazing occurs as a result of expansion and contraction. Since the body and the glaze have different compositions, it is necessary to regulate the thermal expansion of the two. The glaze should always have a lower thermal expansion than the body so that during the glost (glaze) firing, the body "shrinks" more than the glaze, pulling in or compressing the glaze. Glaze is at its strongest when compressed. If the proper balance is not reached, the glaze will be weaker and consequently more prone to crazing under the expansion associated with heat application.

      A second cause of crazing has to do with moisture in the

1. "The Great Ouse": History of a River Navigation, Dorothy Summers, Pub. David and Charles 1973 pp. 133-134

2. "The Great Ouse": History of a River Navigation, Dorothy Summers, Pub. David and Charles 1973 pp. 133-134

body. This is rarely a problem with vitreous body systems, for the more glasslike (non-porous) the body is, the less prone it is to crazing. Earthenware does have some porosity and therefore a tendency to absorb moisture. This can lead to an expansion of the body, reducing the compression of the glaze, thus allowing the crazing. In the manufacturing process, a chemical called Dolomite is added to counteract this tendency.

I have often heard craze lines described as age lines. While it is true that older pieces are more likely to have this fault, it is due to the fact that having been around longer, they have had more time to be exposed to the conditions leading to crazing. But, crazing has been found on brand new items received directly from the import warehouse.

Occasionally, crazing is intentionally sought for decorative purposes. It is then called "crackling" and is produced by alterations in the firing and cooling conditions or by using a less durable glaze formula.

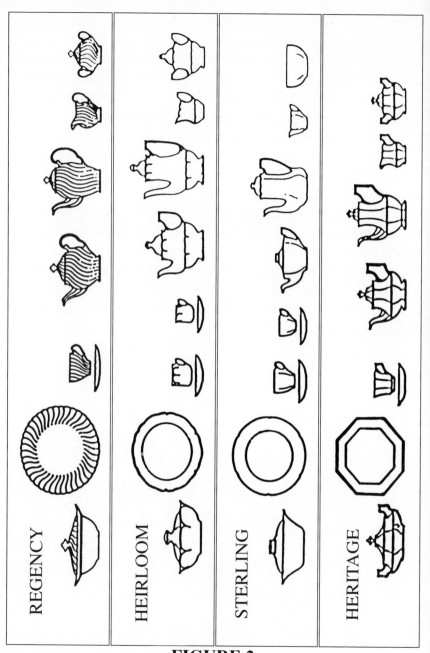

REGENCY

HEIRLOOM

STERLING

HERITAGE

FIGURE 2
Style Names and Shapes of the Principal Tableware Pieces

42

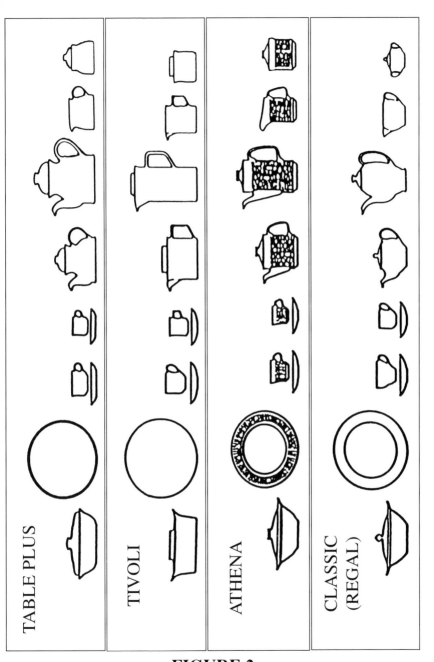

FIGURE 2

Style Names and Shapes of the Principal Tableware Pieces

43

JOHNSON BROS, LTD.
Hanley & Tunstall,
Staffordshire, England
Earthenware, Ironstone.
Impressed or printed
1883–1913 (1883– present)
(member of Wedgwood
Group)

JOHNSON BROS. LTD.
Hanley & Tunstall,
Staffordshire, England
Earthenware, Ironstone.
Printed
ca.1900+ (1883–present)
(member of Wedgwood
Group)

JOHNSON BROS. LTD.
Hanley, Staffordshire.
England
Earthenware, Ironstone.
Printed
ca.1913+ (1883–present)
(member of Wedgwood
Group)

JOHNSON BROS. LTD.
Hanley, Staffordshire.
England
Earthenware, Ironstone
current (1883–present)
(member of Wedgwood
Group)

FIGURE 3

Sample backstamps from Kovel's DICTIONARY OF MARKS, Crown

JOHNSON BROTHERS
MADE IN ENGLAND
DISHWASHER AND
MICROWAVE SAFE

JOHNSON BROTHERS
MADE IN ENGLAND
BLUE JARDIN
GENUINE HAND ENGRAVING
ACID RESISTING AND
DISHWASHER SAFE
IRONSTONE

JB
JOHNSON BROTHERS
Made in England
IRONSTONE

FIGURE 4

CONTEMPORARY BACKSTAMPS

FIGURE 5
DISCONTINUED BACKSTAMPS

FIGURE 6
TWO EXAMPLES OF ROYAL WARRANT BACKSTAMPS

Flat Plates 4" - Balmoral
Flat Plates 5" - Hampton
Flat Plates 6" - Bisham Abbey
Flat Plates 7" - Glamis Castle
Flat Plates 8" - Buckingham Palace
Deep Plates 6" - Bisham Abbey
Deep Plates 7" - Glamis Castle
Deep Plates 8" - Buckingham Palace
Round Coupes 7" - Osbourne House
Oval Dish 8" - Windsor Castle
Oval Dish 9" - Windsor Castle
Oval Dish 10" - Windsor Castle
Oval Dish 12" - Balmoral
Oval Dish 14" - Balmoral
Oval Baker 7" - Hampton Court
Oval Baker 8" - Windsor Castle
Round Dish 12" - Haddon Hall
Round Deep Dish 12" - Haddon Hall
Round Scollop 7" - Hampton Court
Round Scollop 8" - Buckingham Palace
Round Scollop 9" - Buckingham Palace
Sauce Boat - Holyrood
Saucer Boat Fast Stand - York Cottage
Covered Scollop 7" - Hampton Court
Cov'd. Scollop 10" Notched - Buckingham Palace
Coverdish 8" - Hampton Court
Soup Tureen 9" - Windsor Castle
Covered Butter Continental - Kensington
Tete a Tete Tray - Balmoral
Sandwich Tray - Windsor Castle

FIGURE 7
"ROYAL HOMES OF BRITAIN" PIECE LIST

Fruit Saucer 4" - Caernarvon
Rim Fruit - Sandringham House
Oatmeal Bowl - Sandringham
Pickle - York Cottage & Sandringham
Cream Soup/Stand - Kensington Palace
Irish Cups & Saucer TALL or LOW - Caernarvon Castle
London Cup & Saucer TALL or LOW - Caernarvon Castle
A.D. Coffee Cup & Saucer No. 6 - Windsor Castle
Teapots 24s - Hampton Court
Teapots 30s - Haddon Hall
Teapot Individual - Windsor Castle
Coffeepots 24s - Bisham Abbey
Coffeepots 30s - Bisham Abbey
Coffeepot Individual - Windsor Castle
Covered Sugars 30s - Windsor Castle
Covered Sugar Individual - Windsor Castle
Individual Cafe Sugar Bowl - Holyrood
Creams 30s - Kensington
Cream Individual - Kensington
Bread & Butter Plate - Glamis
Eggcups Single - Windsor Castle
Eggcups Double - Windsor Castle
Eggcups Footless Border - (No scene)
Jugs Uncovered 24s - Hampton Court
Jugs Uncovered 30s - Sandringham
Jugs Uncovered 36s - Caernarvon Castle
Jugs Uncovered 42s - Windsor Castle
Bowls 36s - Windsor Castle
Bowls 42s - Windsor Castle
ButterPad - Windsor Castle

FIGURE 7
"ROYAL HOMES OF BRITAIN" PIECE LIST

5 Piece Place Setting	Oval Vegetable Bowl
20 Piece Set	Covered Vegetable Bowl
5 Piece Completer	Covered Sugar
Dinner Plate	Creamer
Bread & Butter Plate	Gravy Boat
Teacup	Gravy Boat Stand
Tea Saucer	Teapot
Square Cereal	Coffee Pot
Round Cereal	Covered Butter
Fruit Saucer	Salt & Pepper
Rim Soup/Pasta Bowl	Pitcher/Jug 24 oz.
Coupe Soup	Soup Tureen
Footed Cereal	Tureen Std./Chop Plate 12"
Square Salad	Demi-Tasse Cup & Saucer
Round Salad	Candlestick
Luncheon Plate	Sandwich Tray
Buffet Plate	3-Part Relish
Coffee Mug 9 oz.	Individual Tree Relish
Small Platter 12"	2-Tier Plate
Medium Platter 14"	8 Piece Coaster Set
Large Platter 16"	Jumbo Cup & Saucer
Turkey Platter 20½	Clock
Round Vegetable Bowl	Cake Plate & Server

FIGURE 8

Current piece list in the United States. Not all pieces available in all patterns.

Picture on the small (12") platter of *"Old Britain Castles"*.

FIGURE 9

49

NOTES

CHAPTER VI

FLOW BLUE

Flowing blue, now commonly called *Flow Blue,* is a decorating style characterized by a blue design with a smudged or blurred appearance. It is found on all types of better pottery from stoneware to porcelain, and is usually an underglaze design although onglaze does occur. It is quite striking in appearance with its deep blue coloring on a white background, often further decorated with touches of gold. The style originated in the Staffordshire area of England around 1800, and Josiah Wedgwood is credited with its early development.

The development of the technique for the production of Flow Blue was not an accident but a positive attempt to solve a problem resulting from two earlier discoveries in the pottery making process. The first of these earlier discoveries was underglaze designs. For many centuries the Chinese had been doing underglaze designs on their porcelains, always hand painted and always in blue. The blue coloring, obtained from cobalt, was the only color used because it was the only color that would tolerate the high temperatures of the glaze firing. In other parts of the world, designs were painted on the surface of the glaze, a much inferior technique, for surface painting is much more readily worn by handling and washing than that which is protected by a glass-like seal. Eventually, processes for underglaze decorating were developed worldwide, but cobalt blue was the only color used until the mid 1800's, when other heat tolerant paints and colors were found.

The second of the earlier advances which led to the Flow Blue technique was the development of transfer printing. (See Chapter III, Finishing and Decorating). Transfer patterns are applied in sections by hand around the edges and along the sides of the various pieces. If this process is not done precisely, the seams where the sections join are noticeable. This is especially true where the last section applied meets the first section applied. The technique of "bleeding" colors tends to cover up these deficiencies as well as having a natural beauty in itself.

This paint flowing reaction results from a group of chemicals placed in the saggers (holding racks) during the glazing process, namely, saltpeter, borax, and white lead. As mentioned above, cobalt blue was the only color used until other heat tolerant colors were discovered, and flow pieces in green, purple, and sepia can be found today, though in far lesser quantities.

The technique for Flow Blue began as a necessity to cover up a problem, but in time this style became very popular for its own decorative appeal. The peak years for production were the mid 1800's through the early 1900's, and the American market was particularly strong for these wares. In order to satisfy the demand, hundreds of potters joined the trend. Johnson Brothers, too, was a producer throughout its early years but discontinued this line of manufacture in the 1920's.

In preparing this Pattern Directory of Johnson Brothers Dinnerware, I have purposely excluded the Flow Blue patterns with the exception of this one chapter. Flow Blue is a collectible unto itself, and many dealers specialize in just that, ignoring the lines of manufacturers and concentrating on the Flow Blue style completely. As a highly collectible commodity, the prices commanded by these Johnson Brothers pieces far surpass the price range of the regular, non-flow patterns. Consequently, I would refer those readers wanting information on this group of Johnson Brothers patterns to seek out publications and dealers specializing in this type of thing. I will, however, offer a listing of the Flow Blue patterns manufactured by Johnson Brothers which I have encountered in the past, some first hand, others only as names in books. None of these patterns are in my stock.

Johnson Brothers Flow Blue Patterns

Andorra

Argyle

Astoria

Brooklyn

Claremont

Coral

Del Monte

Dorothy

Eclipse

Florida

Georgia

Holland

Jewel

Kenworth

Mentone

Mongolia

Normandy

Oregon

Oxford

Peach/Peach Royal

Persian

Princeton

Richmond

Savoy

St. Louis

Sterling

Tulip

Turin

Venetian

Warwick

CHAPTER VII

SUGGESTED PRICING

Without a doubt, this chapter is the most difficult to write. Since there has been so little information on Johnson Brothers patterns in the past, the price variations on these pieces have been extreme. It is not unusual to find the same piece of the same pattern in the same condition at the same flea market with a variation as high as 500%. It concerns me that I am now going to put down some figures that a few dealers will agree with, but a much larger number will be divided equally on the "too low" and "too high" sides.

My initial figures are based on the suggested retail prices for the current Johnson Brothers patterns. Several years ago when I first began to build my replacement service business, I had very little knowledge as to the age, popularity, or availability of the various patterns. Consequently, I developed a price list which valued all printed or colored patterns equally. The all-white patterns were valued at 50% of the retail price of the printed ones. Thus, all dinner plates were the same price, all cups were the same price, and so on. Which pattern did not matter. The price was set according to the piece. Occasionally, my list had to be updated to keep up with rising costs, but the principle of uniform piece pricing remained as did the use of current pattern pricing as a guide.

As time has passed, I have learned a great deal about the need for variation in pricing on these patterns. Age is one factor and with this book, much of the dating is available for the first time. But contrary to the usual thinking of the antique dealer, an older Johnson Brothers pattern is not an automatic indication of a higher price tag. With few exceptions, it has been my experience that patterns retired in the last 50 years are much more in demand than the earlier ones.

Pattern popularity and availability are the primary considerations in pricing these wares. There are a few patterns which I have found to be in great demand, but in exceedingly short supply, all over the country (based on my customer requests). These patterns include *"Tally Ho"*, *"Wild Turkeys"*, and *"Harvest Fruit"*. By demand alone, these patterns should command a substantial additional premium. There are several other patterns I have found to be eligible for an additional premium, but this could vary from dealer to dealer and from area to area. In this latter group I would place *"Historic America"* (all colors), *"Strawberry Fair"*, *"Tulip Time"* (blue and white), *"English Chippendale"* (all colors), *"Persian Tulip"*, and *"Twelve Days of Christmas"*.

To list individual prices on all of the pieces in all of the patterns would require several volumes. Consequently, I have devised a simple "+" and "-" system to guide the dealer in pricing. My 1993 Price List is shown in *Figure 10 on pg. 58*. In the Identification Section of this book I have used the word "Base" to indicate the figures on this Price List. Most of the Johnson Brothers patterns can be priced accordingly. On certain patterns, a "+" or "-" symbol can be seen, suggesting an increase or a decrease in the pricing of that particular pattern. The "-" symbol usually represents an all-white pattern which typically is less costly than a decorated one. Most of these white patterns can be priced between 50% and 75% of the Base price, although two of the more recent ones, *"Richmond"* and *"Old English White"* run slightly higher.

The "+" and "++" symbols have been placed on those patterns which I have found to be much in demand but difficult to locate. Some of them are older, for an older pattern can command a higher price if it is exceptional in design and color. But most of them are quite recent, having been discontinued in the last 50 years. One pattern, *"Coaching Scenes"*, is still in production although routine export to the United States has been discontinued. A "++" symbol warrants an even greater increase. Dealers everywhere will soon find that these patterns are requested by many but rarely found for sale.

One other factor to be considered in pricing concerns those patterns which have been in production over a period of years. In some cases, such as *"Old Britain Castles"* - Pink, the earliest pieces are already 60 years old, but since the pattern is still being produced, some pieces are brand new. In cases such as this, the greater demand, and consequently, the greater value, will be on the older pieces, for the customer who is interested in new pieces can easily locate them in the local stores and does not seek out the antique dealer or flea marketer for help. Often the backstamp can be used as a guide (See Chapt. V) but in addition, the dealer can learn through experience how to recognize older pieces. Older pieces are thinner, more delicate in appearance, and often smaller in size than the newer ones. The surface has a soft patina rather than the high gloss of the new, and often the decorating is more extensive and meticulously applied. The design will extend to the very edges of the piece without a rim of body color showing. Older cups may have inside decoration, as well as outside, and some design may be included on the outside of the cup handle. On newer pieces, both of these areas are more likely to be plain. In a few patterns actual body color changes were made at some point during the years. An example of this is *"Indian Tree"*. Originally, *"Indian Tree"* was produced on a pareek (off-white) background. But, in the 80's, the background color was changed to white. Lastly, style changes are occasionally made during the production cycle. An example of this is *"Old Britain Castles"*. Square salad plates and cereal bowls were produced during the early years of this pattern, but today, only the round versions are available in the new.

There is little doubt in my mind that the value of this book will be as a pattern guide rather than a price guide. But, if the dealer will allow some flexibility in applying these guidelines, a fair and workable price can be reached. We all learned early on that an item is worth only what the customer will pay regardless of what the book says.

MARFINE ANTIQUES

Dinner Plate	$14.00
Luncheon Plate (9")	12.00
Salad Plate (Square or Round)	10.00
Bread & Butter Plate	6.00
Buffet Plate (10½" to 11")	20.00
Tea Cup	10.00
Tea Saucer	5.00
Berry/Fruit	8.00
Cereal/Soup (Square, Round or Lug)	10.00
Rimmed Soup	14.00
7" Soup (Square or Round)	12.00
Sugar and Cover	40.00
Sugar without Cover	30.00
Creamer	30.00
Vegetable - Oval	30.00
Vegetable - Round	25.00
Platter up to 12" (Small)	35.00
Platter (12"-14") (Medium)	45.00
Platter (14" plus) (Large)	60.00 and up
Sauceboat/Gravy	40.00
Sauceboat Base/Relish	20.00
Coffee Mug	15.00
Coaster	6.00
Teapot or Coffeepot	70.00 and up
Covered Vegetable	80.00 and up
Covered Butter	50.00 and up
Salt & Pepper Set	40.00 and up
Chop/Cake Plate (12")	50.00 and up
Eggcup	12.00
Pitcher/Jug	45.00
Jumbo Cup and Saucer	30.00
Turkey Platter (20½")	200.00 and up
Tureen	200.00 and up

*Special or unusual pieces are individually priced.
** These prices do not apply to Flow Blue patterns.(See Chapt.VI)

FIGURE 10: 1993 PRICE LIST

CHAPTER VIII

PATTERN IDENTIFICATION

The Pattern Identification Section of this book consists of two parts, the photographs and the "bits and pieces" of information on the various patterns.

The photographs in the first section are grouped according to color, style, or subject rather than by age or alphabetical order. I felt that this arrangement would have many advantages as a reference tool. The decorator who needs wall pieces (or even a set) in a particular color would find this most useful. The customer who would like to start a set and who tends towards a particular type of design (e.g. florals, scenes, country) would appreciate seeing all such patterns grouped together. And for the individual who has a definite pattern in mind but does not know the name, this arrangement would be ideal, for normally such a person has some idea of the design. The listing of categories for the photographs is as follows:

Blue is Basic
Pink is Pretty
Sensational Scenes
Familiar Favorites
Fantastic Florals
Country Casual
White & Nearly White
Holiday/Wildlife
Contemporary
Whimsical
Golden Oldies
Unidentified

Lastly, I felt that this arrangement would simplify future additions to this book, for a photo could easily be placed in its catagory without disrupting those already there.

The pattern information section is arranged in the traditional alphabetical order. The patterns are numbered, named, and then supplied with the most essential information all on one line. Following the pattern name is the identification of the photography section where the pattern is portrayed. This is often in abbreviated form such as "Blue" for "Blue is Basic", "Scenes" for "Sensational Scenes", "Oldies" for "Golden Oldies", etc. Occasionally, a NA will be seen. This represents "Not Available". Since only plates were photographed for this section, there are many patterns in which many pieces were found so that the pattern could be identified, but unfortunately, no plates were included. In a few of the instances, the pattern is so new that though the plate is currently on hand, it was received too late for the last photographic session.

Following the photo location is the dating. When the exact dates from the beginning to the end of production are known, it is written as two numbers separated by a hyphen. The 19's representing the 20th Century have been left off. Thus, 57-74 means that a pattern was begun in 1957 and discontinued in 1974. In some of the earlier patterns where records are no longer available, an exact date could not be specified. Based on the decorating style and the backstamp, only an "educated guess" could be made. In these instances the dealer will find markings such as "Pre-1930" (before) 1930 or "Circa 1900" (around the turn of the century).

The last grouping is the price guide. As explained in Chapter VII, the word "Base" represents the figures on my 1993 Price List. A further symbol of a "+" or "-" sign indicates to the dealer that either an increase or a decrease in pricing is advised.

If any further information concerning a pattern is known, that data is centered below the first line. In those patterns in which different designs are depicted on various pieces, the listing of pieces and naming of the designs is not complete. In some cases, the listing includes only those few pieces which have been found to date. In other cases, the known list is so long that only a sampling of pieces and designs is given.

Most dealers will be surprised to learn of the many color variations on several of the patterns. An example of this is *"Old Britain Castles"*. The blue, pink, lavender, and brown multicolor are well known here in the States, but very few have had the opportunity to see brown and white or green and white. The usual explanation in these instances is that the "surprise" versions were sold in other parts of the world, but not in the United States.

As mentioned in the Foreword, the patterns included in this book are those which have been found and identified to date and are only a fraction of the total number of patterns produced. Exactly how many are "out there" is not known, but it is likely to be hundreds. The following names are a listing of those patterns that have come to my attention with little or no information other than the name. The search is ongoing. Given a little more time and "umpteen" walks down the miles of aisles at Flea Markets and Antique Fairs, the number of identified and cataloged patterns should continue to grow.

UNIDENTIFIED, UNVERIFIED, OR UNCATEGORIZED PATTERNS

Azalea	Chevreuse	English Country Life
Bagatelle	Classic White	English Gardens
Baroda	Colonial	Ermine
Belford	Columbia	Evangeline
Berry Branch	Contessa	Fancy Free
Blue Cloud	Convolvulus	Finlandia
Blue Ice	County Clare	Fjord
Bordeaux - Old	Dartmouth	Fleur L' Orange
Carnation	Desert Sand	Florentine
Castle Story	Dreamtown	Forget Me Not
Chadwell	Early Dawn	Gossamer
Charleston Garden	Ellastone	Grafton

cont. on next page

Granada
Hague
Havana
Heirloom
Henley
Horten
Indigo
Jacobean
Josephine
King's Road
Kyoto
Leighton
Lexington
Lombardy
Lorraine
Lothair
Lotus
Madras
Marjorie
Marlboro
McDonald's Farm
Minorca

Misty Morning
Mongolia
Montpellier
Montrose
Neighbors
Old English Chintz
Old English Clover
Old English Trellis
Patchwork Farms
Peach Blossom
Penache
Petunia
Pink Garland
Pink Kenmore
Primrose
Raleigh
Regis
Retford
Rodeo
Rosedale
Rosemary
Rouen

Roulette
Royal Homes
Ruth
St. Regis
Sandalwood
Sierra
Simplicity
Sirocco
Stanhope
Straw Market
Sultana
Sunrise
Sylvan
Tea Leaf
Tokio
Turin
Valencia Lace
Verona
Villiers
White Rose
Windsor Flowers

Blue is Basic

Indies

Persian Tulip

Elizabeth

Elizabeth

Willow

Old Britain Castles

Historic America

Old London

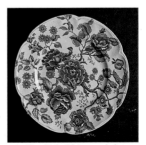

English Chippendale

Old Bradbury

Old Mill

Coaching Scenes

Wiltshire

Tulip Time

Tulip Time

Castle on the Lake

Holland

Blue Jardin

Hyde Park

Deauville

Devon Sprays

Jamestown

Geneva

Nordic

Pontracina (The)

Exeter (The)

*WindsorWare
Unidentified*

Haddon Hall

Petite Fleur

Sonoma

Springfield

Pink is Pretty

Old Britain Castles

Haddon Hall

Pastorale

English Chippendale

Old Mill

Historic America

Avon

*WindsorWare
Unidentified*

Elizabeth

Strawberry Fair

Rose Bouquet

Castle on the Lake

Petite Fleur

Rambler Rose

Mount Vernon

Old Bradbury

Lace

Sensational Scenes

Historic America

Historic America Buffet Plate

Old Britain Castles

Old Britain Castles

Friendly Village

Friendly Village Buffet Plate

Road Home (The)

Heritage Hall

Country Life

Azalea Gardens

Mill Stream

Olde English Countryside

Mount Vernon

Tulip Time

Watermill

Cotswold

Enchanted Garden

Happy England

Familiar Favorites

Indian Tree

Harvest Time

Old Mill

Devonshire

Empire Grape

Rose Chintz

Dorchester

Winchester

Provincial

Bird of Paradise

Pomona

Peachbloom

Castle on the Lake

Georgia

Pastorale

Vintage

Indies

Fairwood

English Chippendale

English Chippendale

Greydawn

71

Goldendawn

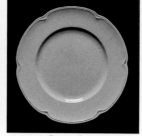
Greendawn

Rosedawn

Fantastic Florals

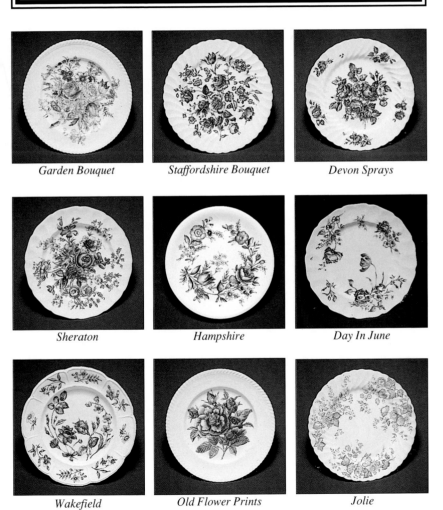

Garden Bouquet   Staffordshire Bouquet   Devon Sprays

Sheraton   Hampshire   Day In June

Wakefield   Old Flower Prints   Jolie

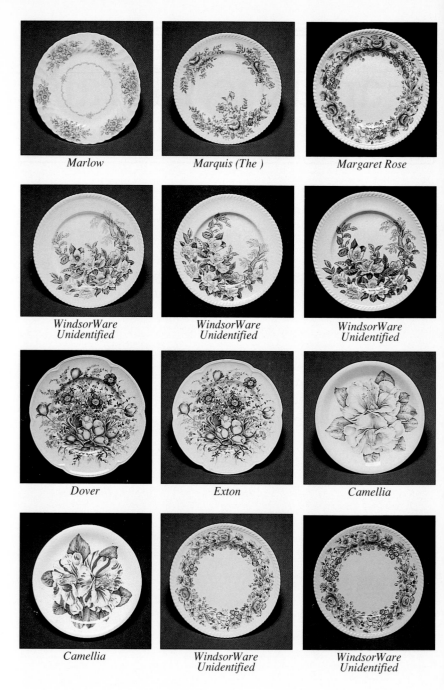

Marlow

Marquis (The)

Margaret Rose

WindsorWare
Unidentified

WindsorWare
Unidentified

WindsorWare
Unidentified

Dover

Exton

Camellia

Camellia

WindsorWare
Unidentified

WindsorWare
Unidentified

74

Country Casual

Fruit Sampler

Arbor

Jamestown

Summer Gold

Hearts & Flowers

Gretchen

Salem

Cherry Thieves

Provence

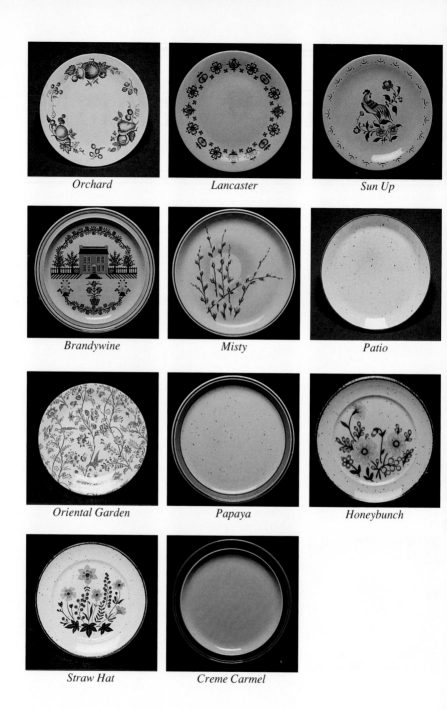

Orchard

Lancaster

Sun Up

Brandywine

Misty

Patio

Oriental Garden

Papaya

Honeybunch

Straw Hat

Creme Carmel

White & Nearly White

Athena

Regency

Old English - White

Richmond

Tivoli

Snowhite

Cottage

Heritage

Sovereign

Unidentified

Eton

Goldein

Encore

Plum Blossom

Arcadia

Kensington

Unidentified

Minuet

Caroline

Scandia

78

Holiday/
Wild Life

Barnyard King

Wild Turkeys

Wild Turkeys

His Majesty

Windsor Fruit

Windsor Fruit

Harvest Fruit

Brookshire

*Gamebirds
Woodcock*

Gamebirds
Ruffed Grouse

Gamebirds
Quail

Gamebirds
Partridge

Gamebirds
Wild Turkey

Gamebirds
Pheasant

Fish # 2

Fish # 3

Fish # 5

Merry Christmas

Contemporary

Celebrity

Danube

Spring Morning

Lynton

Katherine

Vogue

Summer Chintz

Zephyr

Wild Cherries

Fresh Fruit

Summerfields

Eternal Beau

Chequers

Madison

Dorado

Tracy

Melody

Malvern

Thistle

Fleurette

Posy

82

Lemon Tree

Orbit

Auburn

Sandringham

Meadow Lane

83

Whimsical

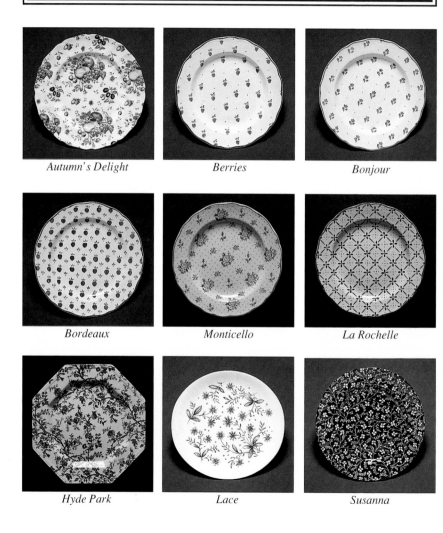

Autumn's Delight

Berries

Bonjour

Bordeaux

Monticello

La Rochelle

Hyde Park

Lace

Susanna

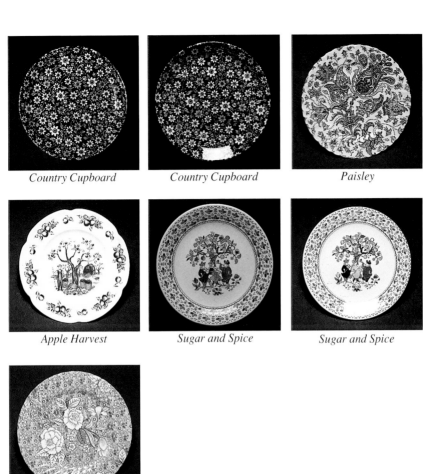

Country Cupboard

Country Cupboard

Paisley

Apple Harvest

Sugar and Spice

Sugar and Spice

Liberty

Golden Oldies

Acton

Coronado

Arcadian

Chintz - Victorian

Vigo (The)

Eastbourne

Victoria

Haverhill

Ningpo

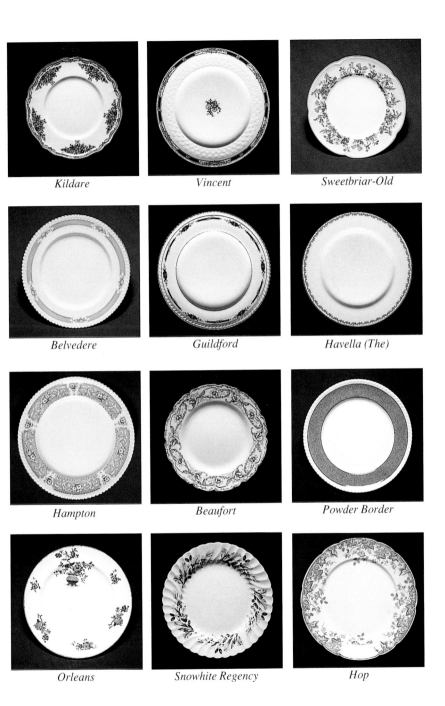

Kildare

Vincent

Sweetbriar-Old

Belvedere

Guildford

Havella (The)

Hampton

Beaufort

Powder Border

Orleans

Snowhite Regency

Hop

Nassau

Malvern-Old

Snowhite Regency

Franklin

Spring Time

Century of Progress

Snowhite Regency

Unidentified

Unidentified

Unidentified

Unidentified

Unidentified

Unidentified

Unidentified

Unidentified

Unidentified

Unidentified

Unidentified

Unidentified

Unidentified

Unidentified

Unidentified

Unidentified

Unidentified

Unidentified

Unidentified WindsorWare

Unidentified WindsorWare

Unidentified WindsorWare

Unidentified

Unidentified   Unidentified   Unidentified

Unidentified   Unidentified   Unidentified

Unidentified

PATTERN INFORMATION

1. **ACTON**	"Oldies"	Pre-1930	# 5	Base
	A "Pareek" pattern.			
	Painted on glaze			
2. **ANCIENT TOWERS**	NA	65-78	# 3	Base
	Produced in blue & white.			
	Various scenes. Royal Warrant.			
3. **APPLE HARVEST**	"Whimsical"	54-60	# 5	Base +
4. **ARBOR**	"Country"	65-75	# 6	Base
	"Old Granite" Series			
5. **ARCADIA**	"White"	65-70	# 8	Base -
6. **ARCADIAN**	"Oldies"	Pre-1930	# 7	Base
	A "Pareek" pattern			
7. **ATHENA**	"White"	55-	# 8	Base -
8. **AUBURN**	"Contemporary"	85-87	# 7	Base
9. **AUTUMN'S DELIGHT**	" Whimsical"	60-74	# 4	Base
	Square salads and cereals available.			
10. **AVON**	"Pink"	60-65	#5	Base
	See: "WindsorWare", "Tulips"			
11. **AZALEA GARDENS**	"Scenes"	59-65	-----	Base
	Unique style. Eight scollops edged with			
	crimping. A "WindsorWare" pattern .			
12. **BAHIA**	NA	79-82	#12	Base
	"Table Plus" Series. Speckled body with			
	brown and blue stripes around edge.			
13. **BARNYARD KING**	"Holiday"	50-70	#11	Base ++
	Limited range of items. Plates, salads,			
	cups and saucers, and serving pieces.			
	Plates are buffet size.			
14. **BEAUFORT**	"Oldies"	Circa 1900	-----	Base +
	Unique style, edged in gold			
15. **BELVEDERE**	"Oldies"	40's -70	#11	Base
16. **BERRIES**	"Whimsical"	78-85	#10	Base
	Originally a Meakin pattern			
17. **BIRD OF PARADISE**	"Favorites"	45-65	#11	Base +
18. **BLUE JARDIN**	"Blue"	81-84	#10	Base
19. **BONJOUR**	"Whimsical"	81-85	#10	Base

20. **BORDEAUX** (Modern)	"Whimsical"	79-83	#10	Base
	Some accessory pieces are solid color red. (e.g. creamer, sugar, cups)			
21. **BRANDYWINE**	"Country"	80-82	#12	Base
	"Table Plus" Series			
22. **BROOKSHIRE**	"Holiday"	90-	# 5	Base +
	Oversize plates.			
23. **CAMELLIA**	"Florals"	? 50's	-----	Base
	Similar to #6, but thinner and lighter in weight. Produced in gray/green and white and multicolor.			
24. **CARMEL**	NA	66-70	-----	Base
	Similar to #6 but thinner and lighter in weight. Different cups and holloware. Large modernistic flowers on a white background.			
25. **CAROLINE**	"White"	88-	# 9	Base
26. **CASTLE ON THE LAKE**	"Favorites"	39-70	#11	Base +
	"Blue"			
	"Pink"			
	Produced in pink, blue, mulberry, and brown multicolor. Buffet plate has different edge (decadon). Square salads and cereals available.			
27. **CELEBRITY**	"Contemporary"	83-88	# 2	Base
28. **CENTURY OF PROGRESS**	"Oldies"	1933	#13	Base ++
	Similar to #10 but much thinner and with crimped edges. Made exclusively for Marshall Field & Company to commemorate the "Century of Progress", the theme of the 1933 World's Fair held in Chicago. Different "Chicago" scenes on various pieces:			

9" Plate	First Fort Dearborn
Small Platter	Field Museum
Saucer	Art Institute of Chicago
Bread & Butter	Chicago Court House
Oval Vegetable	The Forks-Joining Two Rivers (Chicago and Des Plaines)

29. **CHEQUERS**	"Contemporary"	83-85	# 1	Base

30. **CHERRY THIEVES** "Country" "Old Granite" Series		65-70	# 6	Base
31. **CHINTZ** (VICTORIAN) "Oldies" Produced in two color varieties. In maroon, yellow, and pink, and in blue, green, and lavender.		? Pre-1930	# 5	Base ++
32. **COACHING SCENES** "Blue" Manufactured in blue and white, pink and white, green and white, and brown multicolored. Only blue shipped to U.S.. Other colors mainly in Europe. Sometimes called "Hunting Country".		63-	# 3	Base +
33. **CORONADO**	"Oldies" A "Pareek" pattern. Painted on glaze.	Pre-1930	# 5	Base
34. **COTSWOLD**	"Scenes" Produced in blue and white, pink and white, and brown and white. Royal Warrant.	72-83	# 3	Base
35. **COTTAGE**	"White" In style, is the white version of the "Old Granite" Series.	?-85	# 6	Base -
36. **COUNTRY CUPBOARD** "Whimsical" Similar to #6 but with steeper rim. Produced in blue and white and in brown and white. Cups and holloware are solid color-blue or brown. Royal Warrant.		73-77	-----	Base
37. **COUNTRY LIFE**	"Scenes"	59-65	# 4	Base
38. **CREME CARMEL**	"Country" Very heavy stoneware body similar to "Table Plus" Series.	80-82	#12	Base
39. **DAISIES WONT TELL** NA Similar to #6 but thinner and lighter in weight than later patterns of this style. Cups and holloware are solid orange and unique in shape.		68-72	-----	Base
40. **DANUBE**	"Contemporary"	82-84	# 6	Base
41. **DAY IN JUNE**	"Florals" Produced in pink and white, aqua and white, and multicolored.	54-65	#4	Base +
42. **DEAUVILLE**	"Blue"	87-89	# 8	Base

43. **DELRAY**	NA	66-70	-----	Base

Similar to #6 but thinner and lighter
in weight than later patterns of this
style. Royal Warrant. Large modernistic flowers on white background.

44. **DEVON SPRAYS**	"Florals" "Blue"	62-74	# 3	Base

Produced in blue and white, pink and
white, and multicolor.

45. **DEVONSHIRE**	"Favorites"	30's-70	#11	Base +

Produced in brown multicolor and in
pink multicolor.

46. **DORADO**	"Contemporary"	68-70	-----	Base

Similar to #6 but thinner and lighter
in weight than later patterns of this
style. Also, different cups and holloware.
Royal Warrant.

47. **DORCHESTER**	"Favorites"	31-65	#13	Base +

Similar to #10 but thinner and with
crimped edges. Square salads and cereals available. Same pattern as "Winchester" but with different style and
edging.

48. **DOVER**	"Florals"	60-65	# 5	Base

See: "WindsorWare", "Tulips"

49. **EASTBOURNE**	"Oldies"	? Circa 1930	#11	Base

Manufactured in two styles, #11 and
a plainer edge. (Style not known).

50. **ELIZABETH**	"Blue" "Pink"	59-60	#4, #5	Base

Produced in blue and white, pink and
white, and mulberry and white in style
#4. Produced in blue on blue in style
#5. Blue on blue blends beautifully
with "Greydawn".

51. **EMPIRE GRAPE**	"Favorites"	52-65	#11	Base
52. **ENCHANTED GARDEN**	"Scenes"	57-65	# 5	Base

Produced in blue and white, pink and
white, mulberry and white, and black
and white.

53. **ENCORE**	"White"	63-73	# 3	Base -

54. **ENGLISH BOUQUET** NA		Circa 1930	#13	Base
	Similar to #10 but thinner and with crimped edges.			
55. **ENGLISH CHIPPENDALE** "Favorites"	30's-65		# 5	Base +
	"Blue"			
	"Pink"			
	Produced in blue and white, pink and white, aqua and white, an olive green and white. The olive and white style is similar to style #6.			
56. **ETERNAL BEAU**	"Contemporary"	81-	#1	Base
	One of the first patterns to have a matching line of giftware and linens.			
57. **ETON**	"White"	80-83	# 7	Base
58. **EXETER** (THE)	"Blue"	? 20's-30's	# 7	Base
59. **EXTON**	"Florals"	60-65	# 5	Base
	See: "WindsorWare", "Tulips"			
60. **FAIRWOOD**	"Favorites"	62-70	# 3	Base
61. **FISH**	"Holiday"	55-76	-----	Base +
	Oval shaped pieces. Two platters, 17" and $20\frac{1}{2}$", both with scalloped edges. Plates numbered 1-7. Each depicts a different sea animal. #6 was an eel. This was not well received and consequently was replaced by #7. Platters have several of the same fishes as the plates. Cups and saucers depict the fish of plate #2. Oval cereals depict the fish of plate #3.			
62. **FLEURETTE**	"Contemporary"	92-	-----	Base
	Similar to #5, Sterling shape with rope edge. Modern "Old English" style. Plates are oversized.			
63. **FLOATING LEAVES** NA		55-65	-----	Base
	Oval shaped pieces. Produced in gray and white and in multicolor.			
64. **FOCUS**	NA	82-89	# 2	Base -
	The all-white pattern of the #2 style.			
65. **FRANKLIN**	"Oldies"	?Pre1930	# 7	Base -
	Produced in green and white and brown and white. Very heavy. May have been hotelware.			

66. **FRESH FRUIT**	"Contemporary"	90-	# 1	Base +
67. **FRIENDLY VILLAGE**	"Scenes"	53-	# 4	Base

Different scenes on the various pieces.
Square salads and cereals available.
Several "special" pieces produced such
as candleholders, 3-compartment tree
server, and 2-tiered serving piece. In
recent years, a matching line of giftware
and linens produced. Has a set of 12 buffet plates each with a different scene.
These same scenes appear on many of the
other pieces in the set.

Village Green
Lily Pond
Willow by the Brook
Covered Bridge (*Pictured*)
Old Mill
Hay Field
Village Street
The Well
Autumn Mists
Stone Wall
Sugar Maples
School House

68. **FRUIT SAMPLER**	"Country"	65-82	# 6	Base
	"Old Granite" Series			
69. **GAMEBIRDS**	"Holiday"	53-76	-----	Base +

Produced in two styles, round, similar
to #6 but thinner, and oval. Usually,
oval plates have a Pareek background
while round ones have a Snowhite background. However, some round plates with
the Pareek background have been found.
Manufactured in sets of six, each with
a different bird depicted.

Wild Turkey
Quail
Partridge
Woodcock
Pheasant
Ruffed Grouse

70. **GARDEN BOUQUET**	"Florals"	40-70	#11	Base
	A "WindsorWare" pattern.			
71. **GARDEN PARTY**	NA	92-	-----	Base
	Similar to #5 with rope edge. Modern "Old English" style.			
72. **GENEVA**	"Blue"	?Pre1930	-----	Base
	Style not known. Salad plate similar to style #1.			
73. **GEORGIA**	"Favorites"	57-65	# 4	Base
74. **GLENWOOD**	NA	56-65	-----	Base
	Oval shaped pieces. A "WindsorWare" pattern.			
75. **GOLDENDAWN**	"Favorites"	20's-77	# 5	Base
	Colored body not just surface.			
76. **GOLDEIN**	"White"	Pre1930	# 7	Base -
	Classic style edged in gold.			
77. **GREENDAWN**	"Favorites"	20's-77	# 5	Base
	Colored body not just surface.			
78. **GREENFIELD**	NA	70-74	# 1	Base
	White body with multicolored design in center and along inner ridge of rim. Mainly green, orange and yellow. Royal Warrant.			
79. **GRETCHEN**	"Country"	65-74	# 6	Base
	"Old Granite" Series			
80. **GREYDAWN**	"Favorites"	20's-87	# 5	Base
	Colored body not just surface.			
81. **GUILDFORD**	"Oldies"	Circa 1930	#11	Base
	"Old English" style edged in gold.			
82. **HADDON HALL**	"Blue"	50-74	# 5	Base
	"Pink"			
	Produced in blue and white, pink and white and in brown multicolor.			
83. **HAMPSHIRE**	"Florals"	50-65	-----	Base
	Similar to #6 but thinner than later patterns in this style.			
84. **HAMPTON**	"Oldies"	Circa 1930	#11	Base
	"Old English" style edged in gold.			
85. **HAPPY ENGLAND**	"Scenes"	60-circa 1975	# 4	Base
	Multicolored. Also produced in blue and white and brown and white on the Regency shape, Style #3.			

86. **HARVEST FRUIT**	"Holiday"	60-65	-----	Base +

Buffet size plates in unique shape, similar to #10. A "WindsorWare" pattern. Same center design as "Windsor Fruit". Same border as "Wild Turkeys", flying.

87. **HARVEST TIME**	"Favorites"	51-74	# 4	Base

Produced in pink and white, blue and white, and in multicolor, by far the most popular. Square salads and cereals available. 3-tiered serving piece available. Reissued in 1992 through the J.C. Penney Company.

88. **HAVERHILL**	"Oldies"	Pre1930	# 7	Base
89. **HEARTS AND FLOWERS**	"Country"	67-91	# 6	Base

"Old Granite" Series. Royal Warrant.

90. **HERITAGE**	"White"	68-	# 1	Base -
91. **HERITAGE HALL**	"Scenes"	69-80	# 3	Base
		84-85		

Produced in blue and white and in brown multi-colored. First issue was for Sears, Roebuck & Company. These pieces have a stylized SR on the back. Later issue for American Express. Different scenes on various pieces, all depicting plantation type homes.

92. **HEVELLA** (THE)	"Oldies"	Pre1930	# 7	Base -

Classic style edged in gold.

93. **HIS MAJESTY**	"Holiday"	55-	# 4	Base +

Buffet size plates. Limited range of items. Earlier only buffet plates, square salads, cups, saucers, oval vegetables, sauceboats, sauceboat stands, and turkey platters. In 1992, introduced mugs, round desserts (or salads), creamers and sugars.

94. **HISTORIC AMERICA**	"Scenes"	30's-74	# 7	Base +
	"Blue"			
	"Pink"			

Produced in blue and white, pink and white, green and white, and brown multicolor. Only pattern known with a jumbo giant cup and saucer manufactured as a novelty item. (Cup - $9\frac{1}{4}$" in diameter;

saucer - 11¼" in diameter. To Date, found in
all colors but green). Different historical scenes
on various pieces.

Dinner Plate	View of Boston
Buffet Plate	Frozen Up-Thanksgiving
Square Salad	Capitol, Washington
Round Salad	Sacramento City
Bread & Butter	Covered Wagons, Rocky Mntns.
Tea Cup & Saucer	San Francisco, Gold Rush
Oval Vegetable	Erie Canal
Turkey Platter (2):	Frozen Up-Thanksgiving
	Home for Thanksgiving
Round Vegetable	Kansas City, Mo.
Small Platter	Barnum's Museum, N.Y.
Medium Platter	Washington, D.C.
Large Platter	Independence Hall
Sugar	The Clermont on the Hudson
Creamer	Railroad, Valley of the Mohawk
Chop Plate	Flying Cloud

95. **HOLLAND**	"Blue"	70-75	-----	Base

Similar to style #6 but thinner and with
steeper edges. Royal Warrant.

96. **HONEYBUNCH**	"Country"	75-77	-----	Base

Similar to style #7 but much heavier in
weight than is usual. "A la carte" Series.
Only plates, fruits, and cereals decorated,
but all pieces have brown edging.

97. **HOP**	"Oldies"	?Circa 1900	# 7	Base +

Classic style in plates, but unique
shaped accessory pieces.

98. **HYDE PARK**	"Whimsical"	80-83	# 1	Base
	"Blue"			

Produced in blue and white and brown
and white. Same engravings used on
the Regency shape (Style #3) to produce the "Old Bradbury" pattern. Royal Warrant.

99. **INDIAN TREE**	"Favorites"	30's-	# 7	Base

Currently manufactured on white background.
Formerly on Pareek. Change of shape around
1983. Two different styles of cups available.

Square salads and cereals available.
In early years, ginger jars produced.

100. **INDIES**	"Favorites"	65-	# 3	Base

"Blue"
Produced in blue and white, green and
white, and in brown multicolor. Square
salads and cereals available.

101. **JAMESTOWN**	"Country"	65-85	# 6	Base

"Blue"
Produced in blue and white and in brown
multicolor. "Old Granite" Series.

102. **JOLIE**	"Florals"	77-79	# 3	Base

Manufactured exclusively for Sears
Roebuck and Company. Royal Warrant.

103. **KATHERINE**	"Contemporary"	91-	# 7	Base
104. **KENSINGTON**	"White"	65-70	# 3	Base
105. **KILDARE**	"Oldies"	Pre1930	-----	Base

Similar to #10 but much thinner and
more delicate. Edged in gold.

106. **LACE**	"Whimsical"	55-65	-----	Base

"Pink"
Oval shaped pieces. Produced in pink
and white and in multicolor. (Pink and
gray and white).

107. **LANCASTER**	"Country"	65-76	# 6	Base

"Old Granite" Series

108. **LA ROCHELLE**	"Whimsical"	79-83	#10	Base

Some accessory pieces are solid red.
(e.g. cups, creamer, sugar)

109. **LEMON TREE**	"Contemporary"	75-82	# 1	Base
110. **LIBERTY**	"Whimsical"	79-83	# 3	Base

Produced in green and white and rust
and white. Square salads and cereals
available. Manufactured exclusively
for Tiffany and Company. Royal Warrant.

111. **LYNTON**	"Contemporary"	89-	# 5	Base
112. **MADISON**	"Contemporary"	81-	# 1	Base
113. **MALVERN**-Modern	"Contemporary"	88-	# 7	Base

Distributed primarily in the United
Kingdom.

114. **MALVERN**-Old	"Oldies"	Pre1930	-----	Base
Similar to #10 but thinner. "Old Staffordshire" Series.				
115. **MARGARET ROSE**	"Florals"	39-65	#11	Base
A "WindsorWare" pattern.				
116. **MARIE**	NA	92-	# 6	Base
Large multicolored floral pattern on white background. Edged in blue.				
117. **MARLOW**	"Florals"	85-88	# 3	Base
118. **MARQUIS** (THE	"Florals"	41-65	#11	Base
Square salads and cereals available. A "WindsorWare" pattern.				
119. **MEADOW LANE**	"Contemporary"	74-77	# 7	Base
Plates are classic style but accessory pieces are unique and modernistic. One of four "Flower Show" series. Green stripe on rim.				
120. **MELODY**	"Contemporary"	84-	# 3	Base
121. **MERRY CHRISTMAS**	"Holiday"	58-	# 4	Base +
Limited range including plates, salad plates (square), cups, saucers, mugs, round vegetable bowls, turkey platters, sauceboats, sauceboat bases, coasters, chop plates, individual tree servers, and 3 compartment tree servers. Some additional pieces produced in early years. Buffet size plates.				
122. **MILL STREAM**	"Scenes"	60-85	# 4	Base
Produced in blue and white, pink and white, green multicolored and brown multicolored.				
123. **MINUET**	"White"	64-73	# 3	Base
124. **MISTY**	"Country"	79-85	#12	Base
"Table Plus" Series.				
125. **MONTEREY**	NA	66-70	-----	Base
Similar to #6 but thinner than later patterns in this style. Different cups and holloware. Large modernistic flowers and fruits on a white background.				
126. **MONTICELLO**	"Whimsical"	82-83	#10	Base

127. MOUNT VERNON	"Scenes" "Pink"	54-65	-----	Base

Unique style-8 scallops with raised edging. "Wakefield" and "Windsor Fruit" also in this style. Produced in pink and white, green multicolor, and brown multicolor. A "WindsorWare" pattern.

128. NASSAU	"Oldies"	Pre1930	# 7	Base

Edged in gold.

129. NICOLE	NA	92-	# 6	Base

Modernistic floral pattern on white background. Edged in green.

130. NINGPO	"Oldies"	Circa-1900	-----	Base +

Similar to #10 but thinner and more delicate. Painted on glaze. Crimped edge of gold.

131. NORDIC	"Blue"	80-91	# 3	Base

Square salads and cereals available. Originally a Meakin pattern.

132. OLD BRADBURY	"Blue" "Pink"	72-82	# 3	Base

Produced in blue and white and pink and white. Royal Warrant. Same engravings used on Heritage (Style #1) to produce the "Hyde Park" pattern. Later, called just "Bradbury".

133. OLD BRITAIN CASTLES	"Scenes" "Blue" "Pink"	30-	# 5	Base

Produced in blue and white, pink and white, lavender and white, brown and white, mulberry and white, green and white, and brown multicolor. Royal Warrant. In early years, several "special" pieces produced such as ginger jars, finger bowls, etc. Lavender especially hard to find and should be Base+. Different "castles" on various pieces.

Dinner Plate	Blarney Castle	1792
Square Salad	Belvoir Castle	1792
Bread & Butter	Haddon Hall	1792
Oval Vegetable	Ragland Castle	1792

103

	Round Vegetable	Ruthin Castle	1792
	Small Platter	Cambridge	1792
	Medium Platter	Canterbury	1792
	Luncheon Plate	Windsor Castle	1792
	Berry/Fruit	Alnwick Castle	1792

A few pieces have a different scene on each side.

	Tea Cup	Stratford-on-Avon	1792
		Penshurst, Kent	1792
	Creamer	Goodrich Castle	1792
		Brougham Castle	1792
	Sugar Base	Kirkstall Abbey	1792
		Powderham Castle	1792

134. OLD ENGLISH WHITE "White" 91- # 5 Base -

Modern "Old English" style with "rope"
edge on Sterling (#5) style wares.
Oversize dinner plates.

135. OLD FLOWER PRINTS "Florals" 41-late 40's #11 Base

Different flowers portrayed on various
pieces. Square salads and cereals available.

Dinner Plate	Roses
Square Salad	Pansies
Bread & Butter	Morning Glories
Berry/Fruit	Double Daisies
Rim & Lug Soups	Nasturtiums
Oval Vegetable	Asters
Cup & Saucer	Sweet Peas
Luncheon Plate	Pinks
Gravy (Sauceboat)	Heliotropes
Small Platter	Rhododendrons
Creamer	Wild Roses

136. OLD LONDON "Blue" 68-74 # 5 Base

Different "London" scenes on the various
pieces. Royal Warrant.

Dinner Plate	Big Ben
Bread & Butter	Tower of London
Saucer	Westminster
Teacup	Ranelagh Gardens
Coupe Soup	Regent Street

137. OLD MILL "Favorites" 52-77 # 4 Base
"Blue"
"Pink"

Produced in blue and white, pink and white, mulberry and white, and brown multicolor. Buffet plates available.

138. **OLDE ENGLISH COUNTRYSIDE**	"Scenes"	57-83	# 5	Base

Produced in brown multicolor and in mulberry and white. Square salads and cereals available.

139. **ORBIT**	"Contemporary"	84-87	# 7	Base

Produced in pink and white, gray and white, and black and white.

140. **ORCHARD**	"Country"	76-79	# 6	Base

"Old Granite" Series.

141. **ORIENTAL GARDENS**	"Country"	78-82	# 6	Base

A "Laura Ashley" pattern.

142. **ORLEANS**	"Oldies"	Pre 1930	# 7	Base

"Pareek" Series. Painted on glaze.

143. **PAISLEY**	"Whimsical"	70-74	# 3	Base

Produced in black and white, brown and white, green and white, and pink and white.

144. **PAPAYA**	"Country"	76-80	#12	Base

"Table Plus" Series.

145. **PASTORALE**	"Favorites"	59-65	# 4	Base
	"Pink"			

Produced in pink and white, brown and white, mulberry and white, and aqua and white. Square salads and cereals available. "Toile de Jour" on backstamp.

146. **PATIO**	"Country"	72-75	-----	Base

Similar to # 6, but steeper rim. Produced in blue tones and in brown tones.

147. **PEACHBLOOM**	"Favorites"	55-60	-----	Base

Similar to # 5. Design raised under glaze similar to Franciscanware. Only Johnson Brothers pattern of this type found to date.

148. **PERSIAN TULIP**	"Blue"	? 30's	#13	Base +

Similar to #10 but thinner and more delicate with crimped edge. Square salads and cereals available.

149. **PETITE FLEUR**	"Blue"	77-91	# 6	Base
	"Pink"			

Produced in blue and pink. A "Laura Ashley" pattern.

150. **PLUM BLOSSOM**	"White"	65-70	# 8	Base
151. **POMONA**	"Favorites"	41-65	#11	Base

A "WindsorWare" pattern.

152. **PONTRACINA**	"Blue"	Pre 1930	# 7	Base
153. **POSY**	"Contemporary"	75-80	# 1	Base
154. **POWDER BORDER**	"Oldies"	? 30's	#11	Base
155. **PROVENCE**	"Country"	65-74	# 6	Base

"Old Granite" Series.

156. **PROVINCIAL** (New)	NA	92-	# 6	Base

Plain white center with design around edge.

157. **PROVINCIAL** (Old)	"Favorites"	81-85	#10	Base
158. **RAMBLER ROSE**	"Pink"	?40's-50's	#11	Base
159. **REGENCY**	"White"	55-	# 3	Base -

Some early pieces marked "Snowhite Regency". Square salads and cereals available. Used extensively as the base for further decoration. (e.g. Canadian decorating plant in Hamilton Ontario).

160. **RICHMOND**	"White"	87-	# 9	Base -
161. **ROAD HOME** (THE)	"Scenes"	57-74	# 5	Base
162. **ROSE BOUQUET**	"Pink"	63-89	# 3	Base

Produced in pink on white and in blue on white.

163. **ROSE CHINTZ**	"Favorites"	30's-	# 4	Base

Square salads and cereals available. In early years, ginger jars available.

164. **ROSEDAWN**	"Favorites"	20's-70	# 5	Base

Colored body not just surface.

165. **SALEM**	"Country"	65-70	# 6	Base

"Old Granite" Series.

166. **SANDRINGHAM**	"Contemporary"	-------	# 1	Base
167. **SCANDIA**	"White"	65-70	# 8	Base
168. **SHERATON**	"Florals"	44-80	# 4	Base

Square salads and cereals available.

169. **SNOWHITE**	"White"	?40's-50's	-----	Base -

Similar to #6 but with steeper rim.

170. **SNOWHITE REGENCY**	"Oldies"	?40's-50's	# 3	Base
(Decorated)	Origin of decoration not known. Could			

have been the Canadian decorating unit
in Hamilton, Ontario.

171. **SNOWHITE REGENCY**: SEE REGENCY				
(White)				
172. **SONOMA**	"Blue"	81-84	# 6	Base
	Royal Warrant.			
173. **SOVEREIGN**	"White"	90-92	# 5	Base -
	Thicker and heavier than earlier patterns			
	of this style. (e.g. The "Dawn" series).			
174. **SPRING DAY**	NA	74-77	# 7	Base
	Plates are classic style but accessory pieces			
	are unique and modernistic. One of four			
	"Flower Show" series. Yellow stripe on rim.			
175. **SPRING MORNING**	"Contemporary"	?-87	# 1	Base
176. **SPRING TIME**	"Oldies"	Pre 1930	-----	Base +
	Style not known. Pictured plate is a salad			
	plate. A "Pareek" pattern. Painted on glaze.			
177. **SPRINGFIELD**	"Blue"	87-89	# 9	Base
178. **STAFFORDSHIRE BOUQUET**	"Florals"	67-82	# 3	Base
	Royal Warrant. Introduced in the USA			
	as a bank promotion.			
179. **STRAW HAT**	"Country"	?-77	-----	Base
	Similar to style #7 but much heavier in weight			
	than is usual. "A la carte" series.			
180. **STRAWBERRY FAIR**	"Pink"	53-73	# 4	Base +
181. **SUGAR AND SPICE**	"Whimsical"	71-74	# 6	Base
	Produced in brown multicolor and in blue			
	multicolor. Royal Warrant. Was a Sears			
	Roebuck exclusive. Different scenes on			
	various pieces.			
182. **SUMMER CHINTZ**	"Contemporary"	86-	# 3	Base
	Matching line of giftware and linens avail-			
	able. Square salads and cereals available.			
183. **SUMMER GOLD**	"Country"	78-82	#12	Base
	"Table Plus" Series.			
184. **SUMMER SUN**	NA	74-77	# 7	Base
	Plates are classic style but accessory pieces are			
	unique and modernistic. One of four "Flower			
	Show" series. Blue stripe on rim.			
185. **SUMMERFIELDS**	"Contemporary"	85-	# 7	Base
	Matching line of giftware and linens available.			

186. **SUN UP**	"Country" "Old Granite" Series.	65-70	# 6	Base
187. **SUSANNA**	"Whimsical" Produced in brown and white and in sapphire blue and white. A "Laura Ashley" pattern. Most pieces printed with the color on a white back-ground. Plates, saucers, and B&B's reversed.	78-82	# 6	Base
188. **SWEETBRIAR** (Modern) NA		84-87	# 3	Base
189. **SWEETBRIAR** (Old) "Oldies"	A "Pareek" pattern painted on glaze.	Pre1930	# 5	Base
190. **SYLVAN**	NA Plates similar in style to # 7, but saucers have steep rim with molded design for $\frac{3}{8}$" at edge. Available in brown and white and in gray and white.	?Circa 1900	-----	Base +
191. **TALLY HO**	NA Square salads and cereals available. Different English hunting scenes on the various pieces.	57-74	# 4	Base ++
192. **TEA LEAF**	NA Bronze-gold design on white.	?Circa1900	# 7	Base +
193. **THISTLE**	"Contemporary" A "Laura Ashley" pattern.	84-87	# 3	Base
194. **TITANIA**	NA Similar to # 6 but thinner. Unique modernistic accessory pieces. Plate shape not known. Round? Oval?	55-65	-----	Base
195. **TIVOLI**	"White" Similar to # 6 but with steeper rim. Other patterns of this style called "Tivoli" style. (e.g. "Holland" and "Country Cupboard"). Pattern "Snowhite" is older version of this same style.	?-late 80's	-----	Base -
196. **TRACY**	"Contemporary" "Table Plus" Series.	79-82	#12	Base
197. **TULIP TIME**	"Scenes" "Blue" Produced in blue and white and in brown multi-color. (Style #3). Also in blue on blue (Style #5) which blends beautifully with "Greydawn". Blue on white is especially hard to find and should be Base+.	62-77	# 3 # 5	Base

198. **TWELVE DAYS OF CHRISTMAS**	NA	85-87	# 7	Base +

Not a full range. Only plates, salads, and mugs. Some giftware (e.g. candle holders, 2-tiered servers) also. Set consists of four place-settings, a plate, salad, and mug in each. A different day's "gift" from the song is depicted on each piece.

199. **VICTORIA**	"Oldies"	Pre1930	# 5	Base

A "Pareek" pattern painted on glaze.

200. **VICTORIAN CHRISTMAS**	NA	92-	# 7	Base

Christmas tree design on white background Green stripe around rim.

201. **VIGO**, THE	"Oldies"	Pre1930	# 7 #11	Base +

Produced in two styles, both edged in gold.

202. **VINCENT**	"Oldies"	Pre1930	# 7	Base

Textured effect on rim inside of color design.

203. **VINTAGE**	"Favorites"	54-65	# 4	Base
204. **VOGUE**	"Contemporary"	83-88	# 2	Base
205. **WAKEFIELD**	"Florals"	52-65	-----	Base

Unique style-8 scallops with raised edging. "Mount Vernon" and "Windsor Fruit" also in this style. A "WindsorWare" pattern.

206. **WATERMILL**	"Scenes"	73-82	# 3	Base

Produced in blue and white, pink and white, brown and white, and in brown multicolor. Originally, a full range in Style #3. Later, a partial set with only 10" square plates, 6" square plates, 5" fruit bowls, and 8" bowls. Later style sold mainly in Italy.

207. **WEYMOUTH**	NA	60-65	# 5	Base

See: "WindsorWare", "Tulips"

208. **WILD CHERRIES**	"Contemporary"	87-87	# 7	Base
209. **WILD TURKEYS**	"Holiday"	51-74	-----	Base ++

Unique style similar to #10. Three variations on buffet plates-single standing bird, two standing birds, and a flying bird. Both standing bird edgings are floral and lacy looking with insets of a pair of birds every 120^0. The border of the flying bird has fruit as well as flowers but no birds depicted. This border matches that of the "Harvest

Fruit" pattern. To date, all salads, rim soups, cups and saucers, and serving pieces found have had the same decoration as the standing bird pieces. Cups, however, depict a flying bird inside. Platters are available in both border styles. All "Wild Turkey" patterns are "WindsorWare" patterns.

| 210. **WILLOW** | "Blue" | Pre1930- | # 7 | Base |
| | | | | |

Produced in blue and white and pink and white. Previously manufactured in other styles and shapes. Pink discontinued in 1965. Royal Warrant.

| 211. **WILTSHIRE** | "Blue" | 60-65 | # 5 | Base |

See: "WindsorWare", "Tulips"

| 212. **WINCHESTER** | "Favorites" | 47-65 | #11 | Base |

Square salads and cereals available. Same pattern as "Dorchester" with different style and edging.

| 213. **WINDSOR FRUIT** | "Holiday" | 56-65 | # 4 | Base |
| | | | ----- | |

Second style is unique-8 scallops with raised edging. "Wakefield" and "Mount Vernon" also in this style. A "WindsorWare" pattern.

*WINDSORWARE * UNIDENTIFIED * NAMED BY MARFINE*

===

| 214. **W.W. GARLAND** | "Florals" | ?Pre1970 | #11 | Base |

Produced in green multicolor and in brown multicolor.

| 215. **W.W. PODS** | "Blue" | 54-65 | ----- | Base |

Unique style-8 scallops with raised edging. "Windsor Fruit" and "Wakefield" also in this style. Produced in blue and white and in brown multicolor.

| 216. **W.W. PRIMROSE** | "Florals" | Late 40's-? | #11 | Base |
| | "Pink" | | | |

Produced in blue and white, pink and white, green and white, gray and white, and multicolored.

217. **W.W TULIP**	"Florals"	60-65	# 5	Base
	"Blue"			
	"Pink"			

Only instance found to date of the different colors of a single pattern having different names. (Named for English County/Towns).

"Wiltshire"	Blue and white.
"Exton"	Brown and white.
"Dover"	Mulberry and white.
"Avon"	Pink and white.
"Weymouth"	Brown multicolor.

218. ZEPHYR	"Contemporary"	81-84	# 6	Base

"Old Granite" Series. Royal Warrant.

REFERENCES

A LOOK AT WHITE IRONSTONE. Wetherbee. Wallace & Homestead, 1980

ANTIQUES. Ann Kilborn Cole. Collier Books, 1957.

A POTTERS BOOK. Bernard Leach. Transatlantic Arts, Inc.

A SECOND LOOK AT WHITE IRONSTONE. Wetherbee.
Wallace & Homestead, 1985.

ENCYCLOPEDIA OF BRITISH POTTERY & PORCELAIN MARKS.
Godden. Bonanza Books, 1964.

ENCYCLOPEDIA OF CERAMICS. Jervis. New York: 1902.

ENGLISH & CONTINENTAL POTTERY & PORCELAIN. Susan Bagdade &
Allen Bagdade. Warmans, 1987.

ENGLISH POTTERY & PORCELAIN. Honey, 1969.

GRANDMA'S TEA LEAF IRONSTONE. Heavilin. Wallace & Homestead,
1981.

HANDBOOK OF POPULAR ANTIQUES. Katharine Morrison McClinton.
Bonanza Books, 1945.

HOUSEWIFE'S GUIDE TO ANTIQUES. Leslie Gross. Galahad Books, 1959.

OFFICIAL PRICE GUIDE TO POTTERY & PORCELAIN. House of
Collectibles, 1983.

POTTERY & GLASS. 1946.

PRACTICAL BOOK OF CHINAWARE. Eberlein & Ramsdell, J.B. Lippincott.

SMITHSONIAN, (Magazine). Vol. 19 #12, March 1989.

STONEWARE & PORCELAIN. Daniel Rhodes. Chilten Company.

THE POTTERIES. David Sekers. Shire Publications Ltd. 1981.

INDEX

A

Acton 86, 92
A La Carte Cookware 34
Alnwick Castle 104
Ancient Towers 92
Andorra 53
Apple Harvest 85, 92
Arbor 75, 92
Arcadia 78, 92
Arcadian 86, 92
Argyle 53
Arizona Plate, The 37
Art Institute of Chicago 93
Asters 104
Astoria 53
Athena 43, 77, 92
Auburn 83, 92
Autumn Mists 97
Autumn's Delight 84, 92
Avon 66, 92, 111
Azalea 61
Azalea Gardens 69, 92

B

Bagatelle 61
Bahia 92
Barnum's Museum, N.Y. 100
Barnyard King 79, 92
Baroda 61
Bats 17
Beaufort 87, 92
Belford 61
Belvedere 87, 92
Belvoir Castle 103
Berries 33, 84, 92
Berry Branch 61
Bird of Paradise 71, 92
Big Ben 104
Biscuitware 17
Blarney Castle 103
Blue Cloud 61
Blue Ice 61

Blue is Basic 59, 63
Blue Jardin 64, 92
Bone China 15
Bonjour 84, 92
Bordeaux, *new* 84, 93
        old 61
Brandywine 35, 76, 93
Brooklyn 53
Brookshire 79, 93
Brougham Castle 104

C

Cambridge 38, 49, 104
Camellia 74, 93
Canterbury 104
Capitol, Washington 100
Carmel 93
Caroline 78, 93
Carnation 61
Castle on the Lake 64, 67, 71, 93
Castle Story 61
Celebrity 81, 93
Century of Progress 88, 93
Chadwell 61
Charleston Garden 61
Cherry Thieves 75, 94
Chequers 82, 93
Chevreuse 61
Chicago 37
Chicago Courthouse 93
Chintz 86
Chintz, Victorian 94
Claremont 53
Classic, *Regal* 43
        White 61
Coaching Scenes 37, 56, 64, 94
Colonial 61
Columbia 61
Commemorative Plates 36
Contemporary 59, 81
Contessa 61

Convolvulus 61
Coral 53
Coronado 86, 94
Cotswold 69, 94
Cottage 77, 94
Country Casual 59, 75
Country Cupboard 85, 94
Country Life 68, 94
County Clare 61
Covered Bridge 97
Covered Wagon, Rocky Mntns. 100
crackling 41
crazing 40
Creme Carmel 76, 94

D

Daisies Wont Tell 94
Danube 81, 94
Dawn Series 27
Day In June 73, 94
Deauville 64, 94
Del Monte 53
Delray 95
Desert Sand 61
Devonshire 35, 70, 95,
Devon Sprays 64, 73, 95
Dorado 82, 95
Dorchester 70, 95
Dorothy 53
Double Daisies 104
Dover 74, 95
Dreamtown 61

E

Early Dawn 61
Early Morning Sets 34
Eastbourne 86, 95
Eclipse 53
Elizabeth 38, 63, 66, 95
Ellastone 61
Empire Grape 70, 95
Empire State Plate 37
Enchanted Garden 38, 69, 95
Encore 78, 95
English Bouquet 96

English Chippendale 38, 56, 63, 66, 71, 96
English Country Life 61
English Gardens 61
Erie Canal 100
Ermine 61
Eternal Beau 34, 82, 96
Eton 78, 96
Evangeline 61
Exeter, The 65, 96
Exton 74, 96, 111

F

Fairwood 71, 96
Familiar Favorites 59, 70
Fancy Free 61
Fantastic Florals 59, 73
Field Museum 93
Finlandia 61
First Fort Dearborn 93
Fish, #2 80, 96
    #3 80, 96
    #5 80, 96
Fjord 61
Fleurette 82, 96
Fleur L' Orange 61
Floating Leaves 96
Florentine 61
Florida 53
Flow Blue 51, 58
Flying Cloud 100
Focus 96
Forget Me Not 61
Franklin 88, 96
Fresh Fruits 34, 82, 97
Friendly Village 34, 35, 38, 68, 97
Friendly Village, *Buffet Plate* 68
Frozen Up-Thanksgiving 100
Fruit Sampler 36, 75, 97

G

Gamebirds, *Partridge* 80, 97
    Pheasant 80, 97
    Quail 80, 97
    Ruffed Grouse 80, 97

114

Wild Turkey 80, 97
Woodcock 79, 97
Garden Bouquet 36, 73, 98
Garden Party 98
Geneva 65, 98
Georgia 53, 71, 98
glaze 24
Glenwood 98
Goldendawn 72, 98
Golden Oldies 59
Goldein 78, 98
Goodrich Castle 104
Gossamer 61
Grafton 61
Great States of California 37
Greendawn 72, 98
Greenfield 98
greenware 17
Greydawn 71, 98
Gretchen 75, 98
Guildford 35, 87, 98

H

Haddon Hall 65, 66, 98, 103
Hague 61
Hampshire 73, 98
Hampton 87, 98
Happy England 69, 98
Harvest Fruit 56, 79, 99
Harvest Time 34, 70, 99
Havana 62
Havella, The 87, 99
Haverhill 86, 99
Hay Field 97
Hearts & Flowers 75, 99
Heliotropes 104
Heirloom 42, 62
Henley 62
Heritage 42, 77, 99
Heritage Hall 68, 99
His Majesty 79, 99
Historic America 27, 33, 56, 63, 66, 68, 99
Historic America, *Buffet Plate* 68
Holiday/Wildlife 59, 79
Holland 53, 64, 100

Home for Thanksgiving 100
Honey Bunch 76, 100
Hop 87, 100
Horten 62
Hyde Park 84, 100
Hyde Park - Blue 38, 64

I

Independence Hall 100
Indian Tree 30, 33, 57, 70, 100
Indies 63, 71, 101
Indigo 62
Ironstone 16

J

Jacobean 62
Jamestown 65, 75, 101
Jewel 53
Jolie 73, 101
Josephine 62

K

Kansas City, Mo. 100
Katherine 81, 101
Kengsington 78, 101
Kenworth 53
Kildare 87, 101
King's Road 62
Kirkstall Abbey 104
Kyoto 62

L

Lace 67, 84, 101
Lancaster 76, 101
La Rochelle 84, 101
Leighton 62
Lemon Tree 83, 101
Lexington 62
Liberty 85, 101
Lily Pond 97
lithograph 23
Lombardy 62
Lorraine 62
Lothair 62
Lotus 62

Lynton 81, 101

M

Madison 82, 101
Madras 62
Malvern 82, 101
Malvern, *Old* 88, 102
Margaret Rose 74, 102
Marie 102
Marjorie 62
Marlboro 62
Marlow 74, 102
Marquis, The 74, 102
McDonald's Farm 62
Meadow Lane 83, 102
Melody 82, 102
Mentone 53
Merry Christmas 34, 80, 102
Mill Stream 38, 69, 102
Minorca 62
Minuet 78, 102
Misty 76, 102
Misty Morning 62
Mongolia 53, 62
Monterey 102
Monticello 84, 102
Montpellier 62
Montrose 62
Morning Glories 104
Mount Vernon 67, 69, 103
Mount Rushmore 37

N

Nassau 88, 103
Nasturtiums 104
Neighbors 62
New Dictionary of Marks 31
Nicole 103
Ningpo 86, 103
Nordic 65, 103
Normandy 53

O

Old Bradbury 37, 64, 67, 103

Old Britain Castles 27, 30, 33, 38, 39, 49,
57, 63, 66, 68, 103
Old English 35
Chintz 62
Clover 62
Trellis 62
White 35, 56, 77, 104
Old Flower Prints 73, 104
Old Granite 36
Old London 63, 104
Old Mill 38, 64, 66, 70, 97, 104
Olde English Countryside 69, 105
Orbit 83, 105
Orchard 76, 105
Oregon 53
Oregon Plate 37
Oriental Gardens 76, 105
Orleans 87, 105
Oxford 53

P

Paisley 85, 105
Pansies 104
Papaya 35, 76, 105
Pareek 27, 35
Pastorale 38, 66, 71, 105
Patchwork Farms 62
Patio 76, 105
Peach Bloom 71, 105
Peach Blossom 62
Peach/Peach Royal 53
Penache 62
Penshurst, Kent 104
Persian 53
Persian Tulip 56, 63, 105
Petite Fleur 65, 67, 105
Petunia 62
piece list 48
Pink Garland 62
Pink is Pretty 59, 66
Pink Kenmore 62
Pinks 104
Plates, *shapes and styles* 30
Plum Blossom 78, 106
Pomona 36, 71, 106

Pontracina, The 65, 106
Porcelain 15
Posy 82, 106
Powder Border 87, 106
Powderham Castle 104
Primrose 62
Princeton 53
Provence 75, 106
Provincial 33, 70
        new 106
        old 106

Q
Queen's Award to Industry 28

R
Ragland Castle 103
Railroad, Valley of the Mohawks 100
Raleigh 62
Rambler Rose 67, 106
Ranelagh Gardens 104
Regency 42, 77, 106
Regent Street 104
Regis 62
Retford 62
Rhododendrons 104
Richmond 53, 56, 77, 106
Road Home, The 68, 106
Rodeo 62
Rose Bouquet 67, 106
Rose Chintz 33, 70, 106
Rosedale 62
Rosedawn 72, 106
Rosemary 62
Roses 104
Rouen 62
Roulette 62
Royal Homes 32, 46-47, 62
Royal Warrant 37
Ruth 62
Ruthin Castle 104

S
Sacramento City 100
Saggers 17
Salem 75, 106
Sandalwood 62
Sandringham 83, 106
San Francisco, Gold Rush 100
Savoy 53
Scandia 78, 106
School House 97
Sensational Scenes 59, 68
Sheraton 73, 106
Sierra 62
Simplicity 62
Sirroco 62
Slip 16
Snowhite 35, 77, 106
Snowhite Regency 87, 88, 106, 107
Sonoma 65, 107
Sovereign 77, 107
Spring Day 107
Springfield 65, 107
Spring Morning 81, 107
Spring Time 88, 107
Staffordshire Bouquet 73, 107
Stanhope 62
Sterling 42, 53
St. Louis 53
Stone Wall 97
Stratford-on-Avon 104
Strawberry Fair 56, 67, 107
Straw Hat 76, 107
Straw Market 62
St. Regis 62
Sugar and Spice 85, 107
Sugar Maples 97
Sultana 62
Summer Chintz 34, 81, 107
Summerfields 82, 107
Summer Gold 75, 107
Summer Sun 107
Sunrise 62
Sun Up 76, 108
Susanna 84, 108
Sweetbriar, *Modern* 108

Sweetbriar, *Old* 87, 108
Sweet Peas 104
Sylvan 62, 108

T

Table Plus 35, 43
Tally Ho 56, 108
Tea Leaf 62, 108
The Clermont on the Hudson 100
The Forks 93
The Well 97
Thistle 82, 108
Titania 108
Tivoli 43, 77, 108
Tokio 62
Tower of London 104
Tracy 82, 108
Transfer printing 22
Tulip 53
Tulip Time 56, 64, 69, 108
Turin 53, 62
Twelve Days of Christmas 34, 56, 109

U

Unidentified 59, 78, 89, 90, 91, 110

V

Valencia Lace 62
Venetian 53
Verona 62
Victoria 86, 109
Victorian Christmas 109
View of Boston 100
Vigo, The 86, 109
Village Green 97
Village Street 97
Villiers 62
Vincent 87, 109
Vintage 38, 71, 109
Vogue 81, 109

W

Wakefield 73, 109
Warwick 53

Washington, D.C. 100
Watermill 69, 109
Westminster 104
Weymouth 109, 111
Whimsical 59, 84
White & Nearly White 59, 77
White Rose 62
Wild Cherries 81, 109
Wild Roses 104
Wild Turkeys 56, 79, 109
Willow 63, 110
Willow by the Brook 97
Wiltshire 64, 110, 111
Winchester 70, 110
Windsor Castle 104
Windsor Flowers 62
Windsor Fruit 79, 110
WindsorWare 36
WindsorWare Unidentified 65, 66, 74, 110
W. W. Garland 110
W. W. Pods 110
W. W. Primrose 110
W.W. Tulip 110

Y

Z

Zephyr 81, 111

MARFINE ANTIQUES

Johnson Brothers Dinnerware Replacement Service

MARY FINEGAN
Owner
(704) 262-3441

Mailing Address:
P.O. Box 3618
Boone, N.C. 28607

I would like information on ordering pieces of the following Johnson Brothers patterns:

Color (If applicable)

_____   _____

_____   _____

_____   _____

NAME:_____

ADDRESS:_____
　　　　　　　　Street　　　　　or　　　　　P.O. Box

　　　　　　_____
　　　　　　　　City　　　　　State　　　　　Zip

Send to: MARFINE ANTIQUES
　　　　　P.O. BOX 3618
　　　　　BOONE, N.C. 28607

1. If the pattern you are requesting is available in a variety of colors, be sure to state which color you desire.
2. A stamped, self-addressed envelope is requested.

MARFINE ANTIQUES

Johnson Brothers Dinnerware
Replacement Service

MARY FINEGAN
Owner
(704) 262-3441

Mailing Address:
P.O. Box 3618
Boone, N.C. 28607

I would like to order a <u>JOHNSON BROTHERS DINNERWARE PATTERN DIRECTORY</u>. These books are available for $14.00 each, plus shipping and handling.

Shipping and handling: 1 Book - $3.00
2 Books - $4.00
3 Books - $5.00

QUANTITY DISCOUNTS AVAILABLE

NAME:_____

ADDRESS:_____
        Street   or   P.O. Box

        _____
        City   State   Zip

NUMBER OF BOOKS DESIRED: _____
AMOUNT ENCLOSED: _____

Send to: MARFINE ANTIQUES
         P.O. BOX 3618
         BOONE, N.C. 28607

Note: Marfine Antiques does not accept any of the charge cards.
      Please do not send cash through the mail. Either a personal
      check or a money order is acceptable.

121